RIMBAUD

Sebastian Hayes is the author of *The Founding* (Koré/Brimstone) a collection of philosophic folk tales and parables, *The Pomegranate Seeds* (Samuel French), a play for young performers based on the myth of Persephone's abduction to the Underworld, *The Valheil World* (School Productions Ltd.) a play based on the legend of the building of Valhalla, *The Chosen One* (Brimstone Press), a modern tragedy, and two volumes of poetry (available from the author) *Far Cries and Origins*.

Many of his writings on the literary and philosophic matters can be read on his website www.sebastienhayes.co.uk, and he has also recently started a website on the French poet Anna de Noailles www.annadenoailles.com and a combined one www.poetryintranslation.org

Rimbaud Revisited 1968 – 2008
&
Une Saison en Enfer

A new translation

with Notes

Sebastian Hayes

Brimstone Press

First published August 2010 by
BRIMSTONE PRESS
PO Box 114
Shaftebury
SP7 8XN

http://brimstonepress.co.uk

Copyright © Sebastian Hayes 2006-08-28

All rights reserved including translations.

Robert G. Mules, employing the pen name Sebastian Hayes, asserts his right to be identified as the author of this work in accordance with Section 77 of the Copyright, Design and Patents Act, 1988

No part of this book may be reproduced in any form by photocopying or any electronic or mechanical means, including information storage or retrieval systems, without permission in writing from both the copyright owner and the publisher of the book.

ISBN 13: 978-1-906385-15-6

'Esclaves, ne maudissons pas la vie'

Arthur Rimbaud

For Keith Walton

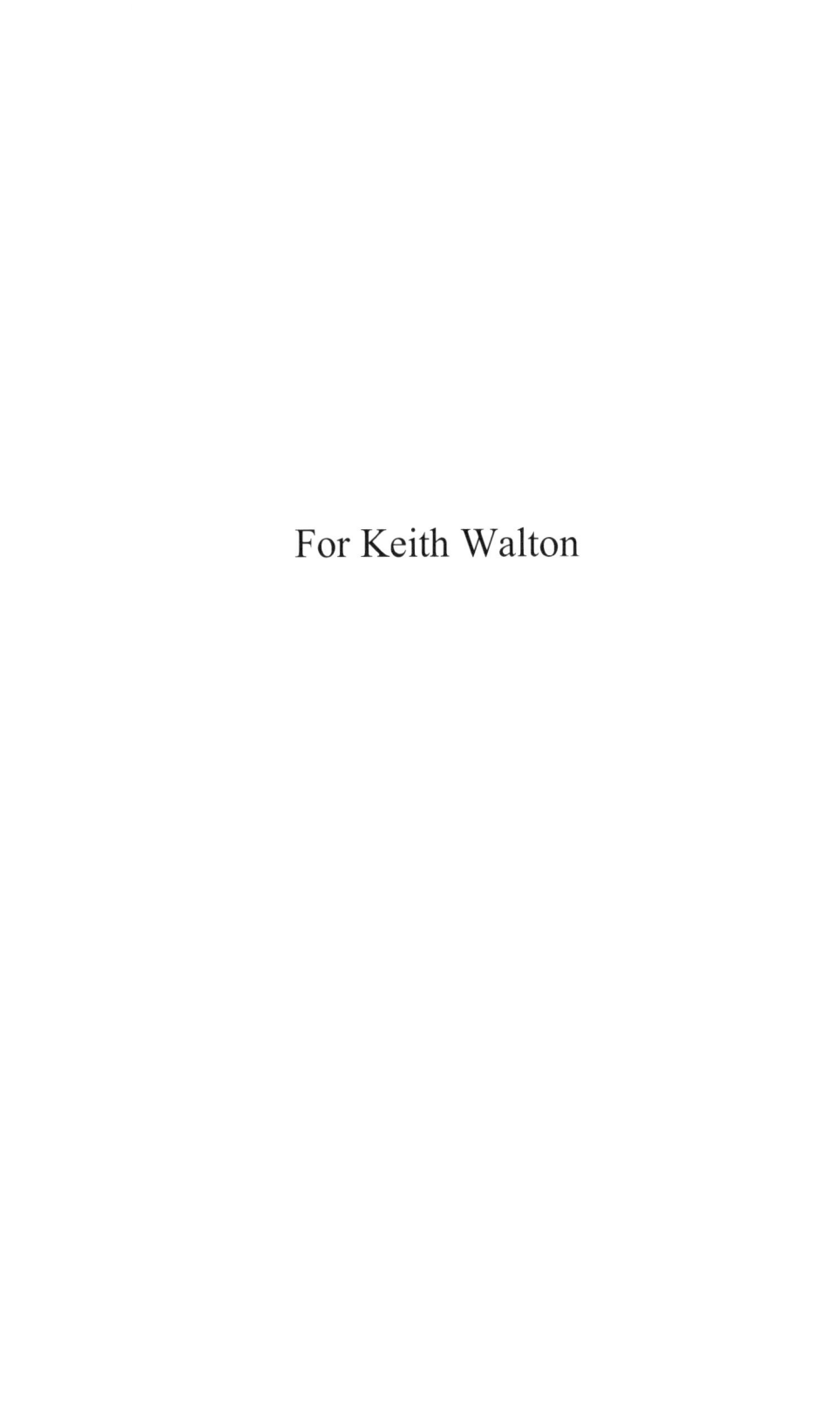

Preface

MY INVOLVEMENT with Arthur Rimbaud began early when I could scarcely read French. It was in part the aura around his personality: at this stage the Rimbaud I related to was the long-haired adolescent rebel who scrawled *'Mort à Dieu'* in chalk on public benches and ended up as a gun-runner in Abyssinia with a young native mistress. He did all this and more while turning out exquisite lyrics like the following which I learned off by heart and recited over and over on solitary country walks:

> *"Par les soirs bleus d'été, j'irai dans les sentiers,*
> *Picoté par les blés, fouler l'herbe menue :*
> *Rêveur, j'en sentirai la fraîcheur à mes pieds,*
> *Je laisserai le vent baigner ma tête nue.*
>
> *Je ne parlerai pas, je ne penserai rien,*
> *Mais l'amour infini me montera dans l'âme,*
> *Et j'irai loin, bien loin, comme un bohémien,*
> *Par la Nature, — heureux comme avec une femme."*

('In the blue summer evenings I shall wander down the country lanes, the stalks of corn and slender grasses will make my feet tingle; in a trance I shall sense the freshness under my feet and let the wind ruffle my hair…
   I shall not speak nor think, but infinite love will well up in my soul, and I shall travel very far away, like a gypsy, alone with Nature — and happy as if I were with a woman.')

   Ten years later, like so many others, I saw Rimbaud as the great nineteenth-century precursor of the Sixties youth revolt, as the original hippie. And there can be no doubt that the experiences and profound changes of perspective that my generation spent twenty years or more trying to assimilate, Rimbaud managed to run through in about three and, what is more important, left a devastatingly lucid record of the whole adventure (or catastrophe).

Today, in my maturer years, I am more inclined to see *Une Saison en Enfer* as an anguished enquiry into the human condition, to be classed with Pascal's *Pensées* or the Old Testament *Ecclesiastes* rather than with the poems of Ginsberg (though *Howl*, Ginsberg's best work, does strike a genuinely Rimbaudian note of outrage and desperation). If we except Villon, Camus was probably right when he described Rimbaud as *'le poète de la révolte, le premier et le plus grand'* ('the first and greatest poet of revolt'). What is disconcerting is that Rimbaud is also *'le dernier poète de la révolte'* since there is so little to add. Rimbaud so completely exhausted the possibilities of rebellion, social, cultural, psychological, metaphysical, that he ended up by rejecting revolt itself as a way of life — this at any rate is one way of interpreting his somewhat dubious North African trading activities.

Rimbaud is, however, in the last resort to be remembered for his writings, not his life. There were other people at the time who led equally, or even more, adventurous lives — Gauguin, Sir Richard Burton — and one of his bohemian friends, Germain Nouveau, looked if anything more stylish than Rimbaud and led a similar existence. I myself met several highly Rimbaudian figures in the formative years I spent drifting around Soho and the Latin Quarter — the handsome, somewhat satanic figure of Derek Dodd, who looked and dressed like a highwayman and committed suicide at the age of twenty-five, springs to mind immediately. But the writings of such people are more often than not disappointing, even dull : their audacity and ingenuity tend to go into their lives, their literary ability into their café repartee.

◈

Rimbaud seems to have originally envisaged *Une Saison en Enfer* as a kind of 'Pagan Bible' — the original draft of the earliest and longest section, *Mauvais Sang*, was entitled *'Livre Païen'* ('Pagan Book'). Now, any 'classic' statement of a theme, *a fortiori* a core religious text, must meet two contradictory requirements. In the first place it must be *definitive* : since it is 'the word of God' nothing needs to be added, and certainly nothing must be excised. *'In the beginning God created the heaven and the earth'* — *'Jadis, si je me souviens bien, ma vie était un festin où s'ouvraient tous les coeurs'*. As it happens, I do not know if there are more than two or three sentences that I would want to remove from *Une Saison en Enfer* — and this is not true of any of Rimbaud's other prose writings.

But it is also essential that a 'sacred text' should be open to a variety of completely different interpretations. A 'revealed truth', since it is timeless, must remain relevant to human experience despite vast and unpredictable social and technological changes : the best of the Greek myths and Biblical stories, likewise *Macbeth* and *Hamlet*, magnificently succeed in doing just this. And so does *Une Saison en Enfer*. It is remarkable how many very different Rimbauds manage to co-exist enabling you to take your pick as it were : there is Rimbaud the adolescent rebel, Rimbaud the romantic, Rimbaud the artist who abandoned art, Rimbaud the socialist revolutionary, Rimbaud the occultist, Rimbaud the religious ascetic... All these personae can be firmly traced back to chapter and verse. In many cases Rimbaud is knowingly inconsistent (but not incoherent) in his attitudes, for example towards love and above all towards God and religion which is why there are abrupt changes of tack within the same paragraph, even the same sentence. Unlike more systematic thinkers, Rimbaud makes no attempt to synthesize, even less tone down, his contradictory impulses but presents them to us in the raw, unsynthesized, allowing them to fight it out amongst themselves. But there is nonetheless a guiding thread that runs through *Une Saison en Enfer*, a central concern from which Rimbaud never departs for a moment : it is the profound conviction that humanity must be transformed and that this transformation must not be limited to one particular sphere, economic, cultural, psychological, what have you, but must involve the whole of life. *Une Saison en Enfer* is the record of one precocious nineteenth century adolescent's frantic attempt, and anguished failure, to find the secret formula to change the world.

◆

A word about the present translation of *Une Saison en Enfer*. Clearly it is not a literal one. I have tried above all to capture something of the pungency and momentum of the original. However, when I do depart from the text, I state this in the Notes and provide the original French with a literal translation.

One is sometimes tempted to give a 'contemporary' feel to the English version — translating *'amis de la mort'* by 'suicide bombers' for example — but I have resisted this. Rimbaud's prose in *Une Saison en Enfer* is not at all slangy : it is hard-hitting but ever so slightly archaic probably because he started his literary career by writing in Latin (in schoolboy compositions). I have thus given (without originally meaning to) a somewhat 'nineteenth-century' version in terms of prose style, certainly not a twenty-first century one.

◆

The present volume is substantially the same text as *Rimbaud's 'Une Saison en Enfer' a new translation together with Rimbaud Revisited 1968—2008* published in 2008 by Brimstone Press. But there were some inaccuracies of fact and typographical errors which have subsequently been corrected — many thanks to Keith Walton, Bernd Wasser and Joy Wood amongst others for having pointed them out to me. Though the actual translation of *Une Saison en Enfer* has been left practically unchanged, I have expanded the Notes in several places and moved around some of my comments.

A SEASON IN HELL

Arthur Rimbaud

****

ONCE upon a time, unless I am much mistaken, my life was a feast where all hearts opened to one another, a banquet overflowing with wine and roses.

One evening I took Beauty upon my knees. Her features seemed harsh and unkind. So I turned her away with insults.

I took up arms against authority.

I fled far away. O poverty and hatred, my sorceresses, it was you who became the guardians of my treasure!

I succeeded in stifling in my breast all hope for the future. I strangled each pleasure like a ravenous beast leaping upon its prey.

I longed for the torturers to come, so I could die biting the butts of their rifles. I longed for plagues so I could flounder in sand and blood. Disaster was my guiding star. I lay down prostrate in the mud. I dried myself in the winds of crime. Madness was my constant playmate.

And the return of spring brought me nothing but the hideous laughter of the insane.

But then, just a few days ago, feeling that the time was ripe and that I was about to make my last croak, I wondered whether I could find the key to the lost paradise — the banquet where, presumably, I would regain my appetite.

Charity is the key! — The very idea shows how far removed I was from reality!

'You will remain an outcast for ever, ha! ha! ha!' shrieks in my ear the demon who seduced me with such delightful opiates. 'Death is the just reward for your illicit desires, egotism and sinfulness.'

Ah! say no more! — But, I beseech you, good sir, do not glower at me with such a bloodshot eye! And while we await the occurrence of my remaining dirty deeds, since I know that you, as the Prince of Darkness, appreciate above all in an author an absence of ornamental and didactic qualities, permit me to detach and offer for your perusal the following stark pages from the diary of a damned soul.

PAGAN BLOOD

I INHERIT from the Gauls, my ancestors, my blue eyes flecked with white, my limited brain power, and my inaptitude for warfare. My style of dress is quite as barbaric as theirs. But I do not put butter in my hair.

The Gauls were the most incompetent cattle-flayers and grass-burners of their time.

I take from them the following characteristics: idolatry and love of sacrilege; the usual vices such as anger and lecherousness — magnificent, the latter! — above all, lying and sloth.

I despise all occupations. Bourgeois and workers — baseborn fellows all. The hand that wields the pen equals the hand that guides the plough. What a century for hands! — But I do not intend to have a hand in it. And as for married life, I view it as the ruin of a man. Begging is too honest a profession for the likes of myself. Criminals disgust me like castrated bullocks: as for me, I am still intact and that's how I intend to remain .

My good fairy must have endowed me at birth with a golden tongue, since up to now it has guided and safeguarded my laziness. Without even having to lift a finger, I have travelled everywhere though as idle as a toad. I have an entry to all households — I mean, of course, families like my own who owe everything they have to 1789 and the Declaration of the Rights of Man. I eat and drink with their elder sons.

If only I could unearth some trace of my predecessors in the annals of the French nation!

But no, nothing.

I can only conclude that I have always belonged to the subject race. And one not even capable of revolt. My lot only ever took up arms in order to loot — wolves tracking a wounded animal.

I have my own memories of my country's history — France, the eldest daughter of the Holy Catholic Church. I swelled the numbers of the rabble marching to the Holy Land; I see before me pathways criss-crossing the Swabian plains, while Byzantium gleams in the distance, likewise the ramparts of Jerusalem; the cult of the Virgin Mary and sentimentalities over the crucified one awaken in me alongside innumerable pagan fairy-tales. — I am a leper squatting on broken pots and nettles at the foot of a wall eaten by the sun. — Later, a mercenary foot-soldier, I am bivouacking somewhere in Germany.

Ah! another glimpse: I am dancing the witches' sabbath with old women and children.

I am unable to recall anything more distant than this country and the advent of Christianity. Visions of myself in the past rush on me endlessly. But always alone — no family; I am not even sure what language I speak. I do not appear in the Councils of the Church ; nor in those of the nobility — the representatives of Christ.

Who was I in the eighteenth century? I only seem to rediscover myself today. No more vagabonds, no more vague wars. The subject race has swallowed everything — the 'masses', Reason, Patriotism, Science.

Science. The latest standard and revised version of the universe. Instead of the Bible and the laying on of hands, we have medicine and philosophy — old wives' tales and rearrangements of popular songs. And then, of course, we must not forget the pastimes of idle princes, amusements strictly forbidden to the populace — for example, geography, cosmography, mechanics, chemistry!...

Science, the new aristocratic principle! Progress. The world is changing. What if it is!

A sort of numerical — or numerological — apocalypse. Attention, folks, we are entering the Age of Mind. A self-evident truth, that; my writings are oracular. My understanding knows no limits, but since I am unable to express myself other than in a barbarous dialect, I prefer to keep silent.

Pagan blood will out! The Age of Spirit is at hand — why, then, does not Christ spring to my aid by endowing my soul with elegance and liberty? Alas! the Gospels have had their day — for where is Christ in all His glory?

I await God with boundless greed. I have been one of the downtrodden throughout all eternity.

Here I am on the shores of Brittany. Look, the lamps are coming on in the towns across the bay. My day's work is ended; I am leaving Europe. The sea-air will scorch my lungs, intolerable climates will tan my hide. I will swim, sprawl on the grass, hunt, smoke hashish; I will drink frightful liquors that scald the throat like molten iron — as my beloved ancestors did when gathered around a wood fire.

I shall return sun-tanned with muscles of steel, my eyes glittering; from my facial mask everyone will know that I am one of the conquerors. I shall heap up gold, become lazy and brutal. Women go for these ferocious invalids returning from hot countries. I shall be involved in international politics. A success story, that's for sure.

At present I am a poor devil, I loathe my own country. The best plan is to stretch out full length on a beach, dead drunk.

What other lands? what other seas? The cross and the bayonet will surely follow me. — Let us take to the roads of this country again, burdened by my secret vice, the vice that has thrust its roots of suffering into my side ever since the age of reason; the ecstasy that lifts me to the sky, breaks, bursts, hurls me down.

The last innocence and the last timidity. I promise I will trouble the world no more with my nausea and treachery.

Forward! The long march, the pack, the desert, boredom, fury.

Who bids for my services? What beast is there to fall down and worship? What sacred image can I smash? What hearts will I break? What lying mask must I put on? In what bloody fields must I tread?

Yes, but beware of the arm of the law. — Better a hard life, first degree degeneration — with a dried out fist lift up the lid of your own coffin, get in, bury yourself alive. In this way one avoids old age and diverse hardships: we Frenchmen are hardly heroes!

— I feel so utterly helpless that I could dedicate my attempts at self-improvement to any sacred image whatsoever.

Think of my self-denial! My charity not of this world, and yet, and yet...

Out of the depths we cry to thee, O Lord! — what bloody nonsense!

Even as a child I idolised the hardened convict bound for his prison overseas; I visited the inns and lodgings he had consecrated by his presence, viewed *through his eyes* the fertile labour in the fields and the clear blue sky; I scented his fatality in the streets of certain towns. He had more strength of purpose than a saint, more worldly knowledge than an explorer, and there he stood, alone, the sole witness of his purity and glory!

Walking the roads in the depths of winter, homeless, half-starving, dressed in rags, a voice clutched at my frozen heart: "Weakness or strength, choose strength. You neither know where nor why you are travelling: enter everywhere, respond to everything. No one will kill you since you no longer belong to the land of the living." By morning I looked so utterly lost, my face glazed like that of a corpse, that the labourers I crossed in the lanes half the time *didn't even notice I was there*.

In the cities the mud suddenly appeared red and black, like a mirror when a lamp is carried about in an adjoining room, like treasure in the forest! A sign of good fortune, I cried, and before me a sea of fire and billowing smoke leaped toward the sky, and the opulent mansions and palaces burst into flames like a hundred million thunderbolts.

Orgies and the friendship of women were for some reason denied me. Not even a companion. I see myself in front of an exasperated mob or standing before the execution squad, and weeping bitter tears to think they could never understand me, and forgiving them! — Like Joan of Arc! "Priests, doctors of the Church, you are wrong to hand me over to the authorities. I never belonged to this people; I worship strange gods; my race is one that sings under torture; I do not understand your justice; the moral sense is absent from me, I am a brute: you are mistaken, mistaken..."

My eyes are closed to your daylight. I am a brute beast, a nigger. (Nonetheless, it is possible for me to be saved.) But you, merchants, you are cannibals; magistrates, you are wolves; generals, you are hyenas; Emperor of France, disgusting old leper, you are a Negro, you gorge yourself at night with duty-free liquor from the stills of the Prince of Darkness. — This people is fever-stricken and cancerous. Cripples and old people are so respectable they deserve to be flayed alive. — The best plan is to flee this dark continent where innocent women and children are given over as hostages to these madmen. I am bound for other waters, the true kingdom of the progeny of Cham.

Do I in fact understand my true nature? know my real needs? *No more explanations!* I must make haste and bury the dead choking my entrails. Shrieks, tam-tam, dance, dance, dance! I do not even want to think about the coming of the white man, when I must crumple into nothingness.

Hunger, thirst, shrieks, dance, dance, dance!

The whites are landing. The cannon! Now we must all undergo baptism, cover our nudity with clothing, earn our living by the sweat of our brow.

Their arrival is the knell that signifies my death. And to think that I had not foreseen it!

After all I have not led an evil life. Days of ease and plenty are before me, I shall be spared the bitter draught of repentance. I shall never know the torments of a damned soul almost dead to goodness whence arises a harsh light like that of funeral candles. The destiny of the prodigal son, a premature coffin sprinkled with limpid tears. Without a doubt debauchery is vile, vice is foolish; one must abhor all impurity. But the clock has not begun to strike that sounds the hour of unadulterated agony! An eagle will come and carry me off like a child to play for ever in the clouds of Olympus, forgetful of pain and sorrow!

Quick, quick! Let us think a moment — what other paths are open to me? Wealth breeds insomnia; the eye of the public would be upon me, money, like murder, will out. Divine love alone holds the key to knowledge. I see now that Nature is an endless spectacle of generosity. Farewell, chimeras, absolutes, errors.

The reasonable song of angel's drifts from the rescue ship: its melody is everlasting love. — Two loves! One can die from profane love, one can die from adoration. I have left behind me many souls who will be much affected by my passing. Tell me, you who chose me from among the shipwrecked, are not those left behind also my friends?

Rescue them!

Reason is born. The world is good. In my last moments, I shall bless the gift of life, love all men as brothers. This is no mere New Year's resolution. I do not expect either to avoid old age or mortality. God is my strength and stay, praise be to God.

Vice holds no appeal for me. Hysteria, debauchery and madness, with whose charms and drawbacks I am well acquainted, all such burdens I hereby lay down for ever. Let us pause an instant to admire the giddy prospect of my purity.

I am no longer capable of appreciating the satisfaction of a vicious beating. I do not feel I am heading for a wedding celebration with Jesus Christ as father-in-law.

The prison bars of reason cannot hold me. I said: God, not science. Freedom plus salvation is my aim: how to attain it? Frivolous tastes have slipped from me. Self-sacrifice and love of God reveal themselves to be inessential matters. I do not regret the century of breviaries and preciosity. Each individual has his own criteria, superciliousness and charity; thanks to my ruthless common sense, I maintain my lead at the head of the angelic field.

As for suburbia and domesticity.......No, no, my heart would not be in it. I am too dissipated now, too fragile. A life of service and apparent usefulness? My own life lacks the necessary ballast, it floats about high above action, the focal point of the present world.

I am become the very image of a lonely spinster, lacking the courage to say yes to death!

If only God would grant me His heavenly calm, the peace that passes understanding, prayer.....Like the saints of old. The saints! Titans! Heroes! Where can they be hiding? Stylites, anchorites, aesthetes of the Holy Grail whose talents no longer find employment!

Everything is like a bad play. My innocence reduces me to tears. Life is a wretched farce and we are the comedians.

Silence! Stand and receive punishment!......*Forward march*!

My lungs are burning already, my temples throbbing! Darkness is upon me, in the noonday heat! Heart, limbs...everything...

Where the hell are you taking me? To battle? Madness, I tell you — I am an arrant coward! My God, they're advancing... My pack, rifle...God damned weather...

Gunshot! Shooting at me, are you? Take that, otherwise I'll turn myself in! — Cowardly bastards! — If you don't stop I'll kill myself! I'll throw myself under the hooves of the horses!

Aah! Got me that time!

— Oof! I expect I'll get used to it.

Forward and do your duty, man, and Long Live the Third Republic!

HELL-FIRE

I HAVE just downed a fantastic mouthful of poison! — Thrice blessed be the train of thought that led me to it! — My entrails are burning. The effect of the venom is racking my body, twisting my limbs into absurd shapes — good God, I can't even raise myself up from the ground! I sit here gasping for breath and dying of thirst, I haven't even got the strength to call out for help. This is Hell, eternal torment! Look there, right in front of me! the flames are leaping higher and higher! I am well and truly grilled this time. Back, demons!

Just a moment ago I understood how everything could be converted to goodness and light — in effect I glimpsed salvation. I wish I could describe to you what I saw — but the air of this inferno is hardly conducive to rhapsodies! — It was a vision of millions of charming creatures, a suave spiritual concert, peace, strength, noble aspirations — you know the kind of thing.

Noble aspirations!

It would seem that despite all I am still alive — imagine what it must be like to be damned for ever and ever! Someone who wants to mutilate himself is indeed a damned soul, is he not? I believe myself in hell, therefore here I sit. The catechism says as much. The marks of baptism are indelible. Parents, you signed my death-warrant and your own with the same pen. — Poor fellow, it wasn't even his fault! For Hell has no effect on pagans. Nonetheless, here I am still alive and kicking. Later on, the delights of damnation will be of a more substantial kind. A crime, quick, so the depths will yawn and swallow me up for good and proper.

Quiet now, calm yourself down..... This is a place of shame and reprobation: Satan himself tells us that fire is ignoble, that my tantrums are frightfully stupid. Enough said on this subject!.... The lies he whispered in my ears, magic, cheap perfume, and slushy music! — And to think that I hold the key, that I see into the heart of things: my critical faculties are unimpaired, all in all, you might say I was dead set for perfection... Pride, the deadliest of the deadly sins...The skin of my head is peeling off. Have pity on me, have pity on me! O Lord, I am so frightened. And thirsty, oh so thirsty! How far away it seems to me now — childhood, the wind in the long grass, rain, stepping-stones, *'moonlight when the village clock strikes twelve'*....The Devil himself is in the belfry at that hour. Mary! Holy Mary, Mother of God... — Ridiculous, this play-acting.

Over there, do I not see some honest souls who wish me well? Come closer, friends, this way... I have a pillow stuffed into my mouth so they cannot hear me, in any case they are only phantoms. No one really cares about anyone else. Keep your distance! I must stink of singed flesh, I guess.

Hallucinations are endless. This is exactly my problem: no faith in the historical process, total absence of moral principles. I had better say no more on this subject: poets and mystics would go green with envy. I am as rich in visions as Croesus, but from now on I intend to be as miserly as the sea.

Well, of all the...... What about that! The clock of my life has just stopped ticking! I am no longer flesh and blood. — Theology is in the right though, Hell is definitely *down below*, and God and His angels on top. — Ecstasy, nightmare, sleep it off in a nest of flame.

What an evil-minded lot they are in this godforsaken hole!.... Satan and Ferdinand are making off with the wild seeds... Jesus walks on the purplish brambles without bending them...just as he walked on the troubled waters of the Sea of Galilee. My lantern reveals his features to me, there he stands, pale and with brown tresses, on the flank of a wave of emerald...

I shall now unveil a whole series of mysteries: religious and scientific enigmas, birth, death, reincarnation, the origin of the universe, nothingness. I am past master in phantasmagoria.

Attention, please!

All occult powers are mine... I am a hundred kilometres away and yet it is my voice you are hearing — I must be careful not to give away too many of my secrets...Would the audience like a negro spiritual, or perhaps the dance of the houris? Just say the word and I will disappear, or dive into the waters to emerge with the ring between my teeth. Voice a wish, name a fancy. I will turn lead into gold, prescribe remedies.

Put your trust in me, folks, nothing else matters. Faith is a comfort to all and sundry, the cure for everything. Step forward, now — that's right, make room for the little ones — so I can take you all in my arms and soothe away your troubles. My heart goes out especially to the poor, to the sick tossing in their hospital beds, and to our dark brethren overseas. I do not ask for your prayers; your confidence in me is quite sufficient.

— All this makes me hardly regret having left the world. I am lucky not to have suffered more. After all, my life was but boyish folly, regrettable in a way.....

Bah! make as many evil faces as possible.

No doubt about it, I have left the world far behind. Not a sound. My sense of touch seems to have gone. Ah! my manor-house in Saxony, my willow wood.... The evenings, nights, and afternoons and days...How tired of it all I am!

I demand a hell for my bad temper, one for pride — and a hell just for caresses; a symposium of furnaces.

I am dying of inanition. It is the grave, I am food for worms, horrible beyond imagination! Satan, storyteller, you will be the ruin of me with your charms. To work, man! I expect a pitch-fork sticking in my side, molten lead dripping on my face...

Aah! how dreadful to return to life again! To set eyes on our deformities. That poison, love, deadly as leprosy. My helplessness, the cruelty of the world. Oh God, have pity on me, have pity, hide me away somewhere, I can't take any more of this! — I am hidden away and at the same time I am not....

It is the fire leaping higher with a damned soul in its midst!

DELIRIUM PART I

DRAMATIS PERSONAE:

FOOLISH VIRGIN
INFERNAL BRIDEGROOM

LET US listen in to the confession of one of my neighbours here in hell:

"O Divine Bridegroom, I beg of you, hear the confession of the most miserable of your servants. I am lost. I am drunk. I am impure. What a life!

I humbly ask for your grace and forgiveness, dear Lord. What tears I shed! And more tears to come, we hope!

Later on I am sure that I will meet the Divine Bridegroom! I was born his subject. — Let the other one beat me now if he wants!

At present I am at the bottom of a bottomless pit! My friends!.....I suppose you're not really my friends... Well, anyway... Such scenes of frenzy and torture, the likes of which have never been seen!....How silly the whole thing is!

And how I suffer! I weep and wail. I really suffer, I do! And yet I am a free agent, it's my fault if you like, I really am the most contemptible of creatures.

Well, I'd better make a clean breast of it even if I have to go over it again and again — a mean and commonplace story if ever there was one!

I am the devoted slave of the Infernal Bridegroom who has been the undoing of so many foolish virgins already. He's the one. And he really exists, you know, he is not a figment of the imagination. As for me, it's true I'm a fallen woman, dead to the world — but they won't kill me for that, surely!   — How can I describe him to you? I hardly know where to begin. I'm dressed in black, I'm always weeping, every little thing frightens me. A little fresh air, dear Lord, I beg of you!

I am a widow...— I *was* a widow, maybe I should say...Oh, yes, believe it or not, I was a respectable woman once — and to think I could end up tomorrow as a bag of bones! It scarcely bears thinking about...*He* was hardly more than a child... His uncanny delicacy bewitched me. I transgressed every moral teaching to follow him into the abyss. What a life! In fact it's not a life at all. We don't inhabit the same world as other people... I follow him wherever he goes, I have to. And half the time all he does is shout at me — at *me*, such a gentle, long-suffering person! A demon, that's what he is: I see him as a demon, you know, *he's not a human being at all*!

He told me right from the beginning, 'I've no time for women — love needs to be reinvented — I hope I am making myself clear. All females want is security, once they've got that they let themselves go to seed. Then follows cold disdain, to be observed in any modern home. Sometimes you do come across women who have more in them and who look as if they could become good comrades of mine, but then they throw themselves away on some repulsive brute...It's quite hopeless.'

I listen to him glorifying vice and throwing a halo of charm around cruelty: 'I come from an ancient race, my ancestors were Norsemen, they used to stick knives in themselves and then drink the blood. I'm going to stab myself all over one of these days, make myself as hideous to look at as a Red Indian. One of these days you'll see me running through the streets screaming. I want to go completely berserk. And don't ever let me catch sight of pearls or rubies, they make me froth at the mouth. The only wealth I want must come spattered with blood. I shall never work...' More than once when he was out of his mind like this, he has grabbed hold of me, and we rolled around on the floor together, I fought with him — imagine that! — On other nights, blind drunk, he lies in wait for me in the street, or somewhere in the house, and leaps out scaring me to death. — 'One day you'll see me with my throat slit — you'd like that, wouldn't you?' — Oh! I can't tell you everything he does when he's in one of his moods!

At other times, he talks in a sort of lilting brogue of the approach of death and of repentance, talks about the many suffering people there are in the world — and undoubtedly they do exist — factory workers and miners, loved ones cruelly separated... In the taverns we frequent, he weeps real tears just to see the people in there, 'the cattle of poverty' he calls them. He helps drunken old men to their feet in the backstreets. He has the sort of love a wicked stepmother has for her husband's children. — And then he'll prance about looking like a young girl off to her first communion. — He claims to be knowledgeable in all sorts of subjects, economics, art, medicine. — I follow him wherever he goes, I can't help myself.

I can see in front of me the sort of décor in which he lives in his imagination: clothes, curtains, furniture. He has a coat of arms, a title, different features. And I can sense at once what would be likely to attract or move him, exactly as if I could read his mind. When he is bored and listless, I follow him into strange and complicated actions with far-reaching consequences for good or evil; all the same, I always feel that I do not really belong to his world. Lying beside his charming body asleep, I stay awake for hours on end at night, trying to find out why he is so eager to escape from everyday reality. No one ever did quite to this extent, I'm sure. I accept that he represents a serious danger to society (and yet for some reason I don't think he will get into trouble). — Does he possess *secret knowledge capable of transforming human life?*

— No, he tells me, he is only searching for it. He holds me spellbound by his loving-kindness, I just can't break away. No one else would have the strength — the strength of desperation — to put up with my situation, I mean, being protected and loved by him. Actually, I can't imagine him being with anyone else; we were fated to be together, I think. His soul is like a palace that has been emptied of all human beings so that no one should see such a base person as myself entering it: this is the bare truth of our relationship. Alas! despite all this I cannot live without him. But of what possible use is my colourless and cowardly existence to someone like him? He doesn't actually succeed in changing me for the better; the utmost he manages to do is to refrain from killing me. Sometimes I say to him, 'I understand the way you feel about me'. — He shrugs his shoulders.

And so, as my sufferings go on and on, and I fall lower and lower in my own estimation — and in the estimation of anyone else who meets me, though there are none since everyone has forgotten I even exist — so I have all the more need of his affection. When he kisses me and puts his arms around me, it is as if a sky opens above my head, a dark and stormy sky, and all I want is to be abandoned there forever, lost, helpless, deaf, dumb and blind. I see us as two little children left unprotected to wander in a paradise of sorrow. No doubt about it, we were made for each other. Moved to tears, we go about our daily tasks. After a penetrating caress, he will say to me, 'All this is going to appear a bit strange, isn't it, when I'm no longer by your side? When you will no longer have my arms around your neck, my breast for you to lay your head on, my kisses on your eyelids. Because I'll have to go far, far away one day. There are other people besides you in the world who need my assistance: I have my duty, you know. It's not exactly an enchanting prospect...Poor little dove...' And all at once I think what it would be like with him gone...the blood rushes to my head and I am plunged into the very pit of darkness: death. I make him promise he will never leave me. This promise he has made twenty times already — it means about as much as my saying to him, 'I understand you, you know.'

Mind you, I've never had occasion to be jealous. He won't leave me, I think. But what will become of him? He has no contacts and refuses to work. He lives in a dream world. The only question is whether his delicacy and tenderness give him any rights in the present society. Sometimes I forget the pitiable condition to which I have sunk, and I tell myself that he will make me strong — we will travel to foreign lands, live by hunting in desert places, sleep on the cobblestones of unknown towns, without cares or troubles. Or again, one morning I'll wake up to find that human laws and customs have changed — thanks to his magic powers — and that society will let me follow my desires and fancies as free as a bird. Oh! I so want that life I read of as a child in adventure books, surely I deserve it after so much suffering — will you not give it to me, my love? He says it is beyond his power. I have never understood what exactly he is looking for. He admits having certain regrets, hopes; but when he says this he is not referring to his life with me. Does he pray to God? Perhaps, I should speak to God in his place? I forget that I am at the bottom of the abyss, and I no longer know how to pray.

If he deigned to explain his troubles to me, would I understand them any better than his sarcasm? Because he attacks me, you know, he spends hours making me ashamed of everything I have ever been attached to, and he becomes quite indignant if I burst into tears.

'You see that elegant young man entering that Georgian mansion: his name is Duval, Dufour, Armand, Maurice, in any case it is of no importance. A woman took to falling in love with that wretched idiot: she is dead now, no doubt she's a saint in heaven. You'll be the death of me in the same way, if I don't look out. That's the sort of thing that happens to us generous, tender-hearted souls...' There have been days when everything people do appears to him like the grotesque movements of marionettes; he laughs and laughs in a horrible way, for minutes on end. — And then he goes back to his mannerisms of a young mother, or dearly loved elder sister. If he were less violent, we would be saved. But his gentleness is deadly also. I am his slave. — Oh! I am half-mad, I suppose.

One day he will disappear in a billow of smoke; but I want to be told about it in advance, if he is going to ascend into heaven, I want to be there to witness the assumption of my little friend!"

A weird couple!

17

DELIRIUM II

VERBAL ALCHEMY

NOW ME. To proceed with the case-history of my own dementia:

For many years I claimed to have all possible landscapes at my command, and in consequence despised the artistic and poetic masterpieces of the current era.

I adored bric-a-brac, Georgian fanlights, stage sets, puppet theatres, inn-signs, two-penny prints; out-of-date literature, Church Latin, erotic books full of spelling mistakes, sentimental ballads, fairy tales, children's books, forgotten operas, absurd jingles, sing-song.

I dreamed crusades, Antarctic expeditions lost with all hands, short-lived republics, mystical movements stamped out by the sword, revolutions in manners, displacements of races and continents: I believed in all possible forms of magic.

I invented the colour of vowels! — A black, E white, I red, O blue, U green. I drew up rules governing the shape and motion of each consonant, and, by employing primeval speech rhythms, I flattered myself that I had hit upon a new poetical language which, once perfected, would affect all the five senses simultaneously. I kept its existence a close secret.

At first all this was merely a pastime. I recorded silences, darkness. I expressed the inexpressible, defined vertigos.

* * * * *

"So far removed from birds and flocks and village girls,
What was I drinking, on my knees, that day?
Around me hazel coppices and misty swirls,
The world I'd known till then seemed far away;

What was I drinking by the river Oise?
Oh voiceless elms and marshes, tell me, pray;
What was I drinking from those yellow gourds?
Liquid gold that took my sense away;

I was an inn-sign etched against the livid sky —
The storm-clouds burst and through the virgin sand
The moisture from the wood came trickling by,
Great sheets of ice, Godsent, concealed the land...

Weeping, I saw the gold, yet could not drink."

* * * * *

"At four in the morning, that summer, sleep held me still. The odours of last night's carnival evaporate through the lanes and meadows.

Below my perch, in their vast workshop lit by the Hesperidean sun, the Carpenters are already astir, in shirt-sleeves.

In tranquil plains of sea-foam, they prepare stupendous canopies on which the towns will paint false skies.

O Venus, leave your pallid, gem-crowned lovers, hasten to their side, the grateful subjects of the Queen of Babylon.

O Queen of Shepherds, bring these workmen their morning flask, so they can toil in peace until their noonday bathe in the sea."

* * * * *

    Quaint and stylised diction played an exaggerated role in my alchemical language.

    I trained myself in straightforward hallucination: I learned to see, without effort, a mosque in the place of a factory, a drummers' school taught by angels, hansom cabs careering across the sky, a drawing-room at the bottom of a lake; I saw monsters and mysteries in everything around me, the title of a music-hall comedy rooted me to the spot with helpless fear.

    I then justified my magical tomfoolery by the use of fantastical terms!

    I ended up by considering my mental confusion as something sacred. I became vapid and listless, weighed down by fever; I envied the beasts their simple happiness — caterpillars who symbolize the innocence of limbo, moles the blind trance of virginity!

    My character deteriorated rapidly. I bade farewell to the world in a series of sentimental ballads:

THE SONG OF THE HIGHEST TOWER

> How long must I wait for it, how long,
> The Time of my Heart's Desire?
>
> So long have I waited, so long,
> The years have slipped away,
> All fear and suffering is gone
> As here in patience I stay;
> Throughout my veins black bile
> Courses all the while.
>
> How long must I wait for it, how long,
> The Time of my Heart's Desire?

Like a wilderness I am,
A garden left to grow,
Myrrh blossoms with the briars,
Lilies, with weeds below;
A buzzing from the skies
Of a thousand loathsome flies.

How long must I wait for it, how long,
The Time of my Heart's Desire?"

I loved the wilderness, charred orchards, faded shop-fronts, lukewarm syrups. I haunted evil-smelling alleyways where I offered myself, eyes closed, to the sun, god of fire.

'General, if you have only so much as a single rusty cannon on your ruined ramparts, bombard us with blocks of dried earth. Direct your fire at the fashionable boutiques and salons! Make the capital bite the dust! Oxidize the gargoyles! Fill our boudoirs with the smell of powder and crushed rubies...'

Meanwhile, a tipsy gnat in the urinal of a village pub, in love with borage, turns to nothing in the light of a sunbeam!

HUNGER

If I hunger for anything, it is only for earth and stones. I feed on empty air, rock, coal and iron.

Away, my hungers; browse on meadows of sound. Suck the gaudy poison of the sly convolvulus.

I lunch on mashed pebbles and the time-worn pillars of abbeys, on boulders left from Noah's flood, and bake loaves with long-forgotten valleys.

*

The wolf howls in the shrubbery feasting on stolen peacocks' plumes; like him, I wear myself away.

Green leaves and apples are asking to be picked, but the spider in the hedge feeds on nothing but violets.

Leave me to slumber and stew on the altars of Solomon; the soup trickles over the rusty rim and mingles with the Cedron."

And in the end, what ecstasy! what science! I peeled away the blue from the sky — it is in reality blackness — and lived as a spark of gold by the *light of nature*. Out of pure joy I assumed the most absurd and far-fetched attitudes:

> "I have found her, have found her —
>   Who? — Eternity.
> She is the rays of the sun
>   Falling across the sea.
>
> My immortal soul,
>   Take care where you stay,
> Alone in the night you lie,
>   Alone in the blazing day;
>
> The applause of the crowd,
>   Take no heed, take no heed,
> Fly as free as a bird,
>   Where your fancies lead;
>
> Hope not for reward,
>   Nor ask wherefore,
> Knowledge and patience,
>   Torment is sure;
>
> Tomorrow has come,
>   And the fire dies low,

> The warmth of your heart
> Must keep it aglow;
>
> I have found her, have found her!
> Who? — Eternity.
> She is the rays of the sun
> Falling across the sea."

* * * * *

I became a fantastic opera: I understood that all human beings have a fatal leaning towards happiness. Work is not life but a way of squandering one's energy, a neurosis. And morality is the product of defective brains.

Each individual seemed to me to require several *other* lives. This gentleman has no idea what he is doing — he has become an angel. That family lives in a dog-kennel. I sometimes conversed out loud in front of people with episodes from their previous lives. — Once I even fell in love with a pig.

I neglected none of the formulae of madness — madness in the strictest sense of the word. I could recite them by heart. I reduced them to a system.

My health was endangered. Horror came upon me. I lapsed into unconsciousness for several days on end, and, on awakening, I relived the most distressing dreams. I was ripe for death and my delirium carried me to the very confines of this world, to the shadowy wastes of Cimmeria, land of whirlpools and enigmas.

I had to travel, to try and dissipate the various spells concentrated in my brain. I loved the ocean as if it had the power to wash away my sins, and each time I left the shore I saw the cross of hope rising. I was damned by the rainbow. Ecstasy was my fatality, my remorse, my curse; my life always appeared to me to be too immense a gift to be sacrificed on the altar of strength or beauty.

Ecstasy! its tooth, sweet until death, warned me at the crowing of the cock — *ad matutinem*, at the *Christus venit* — in the most desolate of towns:

"O seasons, O palaces! What soul is without fault?

I have learned the magic lore of ecstasy, which no one can elude.

There! it is almost within my grasp as dawn breaks and the cock of France bids me be gone.

Alas! I shall never have to strive for it again, for its shadow has fallen over my entire life.

The spell has taken, the word has become flesh and blood, and all my efforts to avoid it have been in vain.

O seasons, O palaces!
The hour of its going hence will signify my death.

O seasons, O palaces!"

* * * * *

This also has passed away. I now know how to greet beauty.

UTOPIA

THAT LIFE I used to lead, walking the roads in all weathers, as sober as a hermit, more disinterested than a beggar, proud of having neither country nor friends, what idiocy it all was. — And to think it is only now that I realize it!
— Nonetheless I was surely right to despise those pathetic idiots who will do anything to get their hands on a female, parasites on the health and cleanliness of our women, particularly in these days when there is so little accord between the sexes.

I was a hundred times right to despise them all, since I have put all that behind me!

Yes, I have put all that behind me since I am leaving for good!

Allow me to explain.

Only yesterday I muttered to myself: "Heavens above, as if there were not enough degenerates down here already! I have spent too long in their circus. I know each one of their mean little tricks. We shake hands, pass the time of day, but at bottom we feel nothing but disgust for one another. True generosity is not to be found among us. But we go through the motions; our social behaviour is invariably right and proper." Is this surprising? Not particularly. For what does society consist of ? Tradesmen and gullible fools..... One should count oneself lucky not to be knocked down in the street, I suppose. But what about the better sort of people, the élite — how would *they* behave towards me ? The only 'élite' I ever come across are a few jovial, embittered fellows and with them there's no need to stand on ceremony. They are probably about the best we can hope for. But they are not exactly easy to get on with !

I came across twopence worth of good sense the other day — it doesn't stretch very far! — and realized that a good deal of my mental confusion comes from not having realised soon enough that we live in the Western hemisphere. We are denizens of the Occidental bogs and marshes! I do not mean that our sunlight is necessarily impaired, the shape of objects distorted, movements deflected from their true course... No, but for all that I seem to have decided to take upon myself all the cruelty and imbecility that the human spirit has incurred since the decline of the East... An ambitious project, you might say!

My twopence worth of good sense has run out already! Mind is stronger than matter, and my mind tells me that I am an inhabitant of the West whether I like it or not. To really live according to my desires, I would have to silence it forever.

So let us do just that! I hereby consign to the devil the joys of martyrdom, the glories of art, the vanity of inventors and the fury of looters; I return to the East, to the original and perennial wisdom. — It would seem to be a gospel of unadulterated idleness!

All the same I hardly expected to avoid all the pitfalls of the modern world. I did not, for example, consider reverting to the bastard wisdom of the Koran. — The evil has been with us for some time already, at least since that world-famous declaration of scientific principles, Christianity. From then on humanity has been playing a game with itself, has found it necessary to prove the obvious, is pathetically fond of repeating over and over these very same proofs — and is incapable of living in any other way! A complicated and childish form of torture which is at the root even of my own metaphysical confusion. As if anything in nature, left to its own devices, would ever know a moment's boredom! M. Prudhomme comes from the same stable as Christ.

Doubtless the fault is to be ascribed to our foggy climate! We absorb typhoid and influenza with each spoonful of watery cabbage! Followed by alcoholism, nicotine, ignorance and self-sacrifice! All this is at some remove from the speculative wisdom of the East, our original home. Why bother with modern society if it entails such deadly poisons?

The Reverend So-and-so replies: Quite true, young man, your basic thesis is sound. But you are talking of the

Earthly Paradise. There is nothing to be gleaned from the early history of China and Japan. — True enough, in a way. I was indeed thinking of Eden. And what relevance has the purity of bygone times to my own dream of the future?

Philosophy has the answer: Truth is not the prerogative of any particular age. Peoples move about but the human condition remains the same. You are an inhabitant of the West but are free to inhabit the Orient of your imagination, as exotic as you care to make it. So, you see, all is not lost, my friend... Philosophers, you are yourselves products of your own wretched Occident.

Take heed, my mind. No ill-considered conversions. Patience, my man, patience. Alas! science and technology will never be quick enough for me!

— But I seem to be nodding off.

If my mind had been fully awake from a certain moment onwards, I would soon be within reach of the truth which, perhaps, even now, is all around us complete with its tearful angels! — Had my mind been fully awake prior to that moment, then I would never have given way to my baser instincts at a period already lost in the distant past! — And if I had been in full possession of my faculties from the very beginning, I would even now be swimming in the lake of absolute enlightenment!...

O purity! lost innocence!

In a single moment of truth my eyes opened to the light of paradise! — Thought is the path that leads to God.

Desperate and hopeless humanity!

LIGHTNING IN THE DARKNESS

HUMAN TOIL! the explosion that lights up my abyss from time to time.

'Nothing is vanity! Believe in Science and forward march!' cries the modern Ecclesiastes — that is to say, *everyone*. For all that, the corpses of the idle and the wicked still weigh heavily upon the living... Quick, quick, over there, beyond the darkness, future compensations, unending bliss...are they not there for the taking?

— Bah! What difference could I make anyway? Work — well, we all know what that's like; and Science is too slow. My prayers gallop, sunlight upbraids my tardy steps...this I perceive only too clearly. It's all too simple, and the heat is stifling; humanity will get on without me. I have my own allotted task in life, and, like so many others, hereby exercise my democratic rights by laying it aside.

My life is used up. Enough said: we will imagine ourselves otherwise and toil no more — how pitiful! We will exist by devising amusements for ourselves, dreaming of monstrous loves and fantastic universes, complaining to the stars and finding fault with the masquerades around us — mountebank, beggar, artist, bandit — priest! In my hospital bed the smell of incense came back to me so strongly... Priests, guardians of the sacred drug, confessors, martyrs...

I recognize in these fancies the results of my putrid upbringing. What of it? All is not lost; am I not young and handsome, my cheeks flushed with twenty summers?

No! no! at present I rebel against death! And work would be too flimsy a covering for my pride, self-betrayal too brief an agony. At the last moment, I shall lash out in all directions...

And then, oh then, my poor little soul, eternity would be well and truly lost to us, would it not?

MORNING

DID I NOT once upon a time have a marvellous childhood, heroic, fabulous, worthy to be written in letters of gold? By what crime, what error, have I merited my present helplessness? You who tell me that beasts sob with pain, that sick men despair and that the dead have nightmares, try to unravel the mystery of my fall and present torpor. For I am no more able to account for my decline than the beggar with his perpetual *Pater Noster* and *Ave Maria*. *I can no longer express myself in words.*

And yet for all that I feel that today I have brought to a close the record of my passage through the infernal regions. Hell...the Biblical hell, whose gates were once opened by the Son of Man.

For me it is always the same desert place and the same night sky; my tired eyes turned towards the silver star, I wait in vain for a sign from the powers that govern all life, the three kings — the heart, the mind and the soul. When is it that we will set out, crossing sand-dunes and mountains, to salute the coming of a new order, a new concept of work, a new form of wisdom, the flight of tyrants and of demons, the end of superstition, and celebrate — for the first time! — the birth of the Saviour on this earth!

Voices from the sky, the march of peoples! Fellow slaves, let us not abuse the gift of life!

SILENCE AND EXILE

AUTUMN already! — But why regret that summer does not last for ever since I am now embarked on the quest for the light of paradise, far from men who live and die according to the seasons.

Autumn. My barque, its masts hidden by the freezing fog, turns to enter the port of suffering, the enormous city whose skyline is streaked with flames and grime. Images of my life there rise before me: filthy rags, rain-soaked crusts of bread, nights of drunkenness, the innumerable desires that crucified me there. Without a doubt she lives and reigns still, the sinister Queen with power over millions of lost souls and bodies *who even now await punishment*! I see myself with my skin covered with mud and pustules, maggots crawling out of my hair and armpits, and still more fearsome parasites gnawing at my heart, stretched out on the paving-stones amongst the unidentified bodies, ageless and senseless... I nearly died there. Frightful recollection! I detest poverty.

And I dread winter because it is the season of comfort.

Sometimes I see above my head beaches stretching in all directions covered with nations living together in joy. A great golden airship glides across the sky, its multicoloured flags waving in the morning breeze. I have invented all possible feasts, triumphs, dramas. I set out to create new stars, new flowers, new bodies, new languages. I believed myself to be the vehicle of supernatural powers. And now, it would seem, I must bury for ever my day-dreams and memories! A brilliant career as artist and novelist nipped in the bud!

I who saw myself as magician and angel, beyond the reaches of good and evil, have been sent back to earth with a mission to accomplish, condemned to embrace the harshness of everyday reality. A peasant after all...

Was I mistaken? Is this change of heart a sign of my approaching death?

I must at least ask forgiveness for filling my head with lies. And now it is time for me to leave.

What! Not a single friend! And to whom can I turn for help?

*   *   *   *   *

Without a doubt, the present hour will be a most severe one.

But I am confident that ultimate victory will be mine: the gnashing of teeth, the hissing of flames, the pestilential moans diminish with every hour. The pathetic episodes of my past life fade into nothingness. My last regrets are no more: my envy for beggars, outlaws, suicides — degenerates that belong to a bygone era. — Scum, I only wish I could be revenged on the whole lot of you!

It is essential to be absolutely modern.

No paeans of triumph as yet: above all maintain the ground gained. That terrible night, wrestling with angels, dried blood smoking in my face and nothing behind me but that hideous stunted tree! Spiritual combat is as deadly as armed warfare; but the vision of justice is the prerogative of God alone.

Nonetheless, I feel we are on the threshold of a new era. Let us all absorb influxes of strength and tenderness, and at dawn, armed with burning patience, we will enter the splendid towns.

What did I say of help or the hand of a friend? My strength lies in the fact that I can despise your lying loves and strike shame into your hypocritical couples; I have witnessed the degradation of woman down here, and soon it will be permitted me *to hold in my arms the truth in a soul and a body.*

April-August 1873

NOTES

TITLE: 'A SEASON IN HELL'

Rimbaud speaks of spending a *'season'* in hell whereas hell is supposedly the place from which there is no escape — in Dante the inscription on the portal reads *"Abandon hope, all ye who enter here"*.

But Rimbaud's hell is not the same as Dante's and in legend and mythology a number of heroes do 'descend into hell' and live to tell the tale, notably Theseus, Hercules and Orpheus — and for that matter Dante himself. By his choice of title, Rimbaud implies right from the beginning that his confinement is not going to be for all time though in some of the early sections one might well get this impression. He is thus writing his account from the standpoint of someone who has already passed through the infernal regions and is about to emerge on the other side. Though we should perhaps never completely lose sight of 'hell' in the literal, Catholic, sense, Rimbaud clearly has in mind an inner, not an outer, state of turmoil. Just as Dante recounts for our edification what he sees and hears in the infernal regions, Rimbaud gives us a more modern first-hand account.

Hell also has an alchemical sense of which Rimbaud would have been well aware : it signifies the preparatory 'black work' which is the first stage in the transformation of the raw material.* In terms of 'human alchemy' the 'black work' is the painful soul-searching which eventually leads on to the complete regeneration of the individual — or so one hopes.

---

* Marguerite Yourcenar has written a remarkable novel about a Renaissance alchemist and freethinker, *L'Œuvre en Noir*. The English title is *The Abyss*.

"Once upon a time....my life was a feast"

French: *'festin'* — lit. 'feast'. Rimbaud has in mind the central place that 'feasts' held in primitive society, being not only occasions for eating and drinking but for the renewal of the fraternal bonds holding the tribe together.

There is perhaps also an oblique reference to the marriage feast at Cana when Christ changed water into wine, the first of many parallels between the transformation Rimbaud is looking for and the abortive attempt at changing the world made by Christ. Rimbaud specifically treats of the Cana miracle in his *Proses Évangéliques*.

But when do we situate this golden era of Rimbaud's *own* life? His childhood was mainly unhappy since his father, who was a Captain in the Army, abandoned his family, leaving his children to the care of an over-strict single parent. And the two years Rimbaud spent on and off in the company of Verlaine can hardly be described as idyllic. All that is left is the brief interlude between college and London/Brussels when he was made much of in literary and bohemian circles in Paris — though they turned against him soon afterwards.

However, as the next section, *Mauvais Sang* demonstrates, Rimbaud also sees himself as a cosmic figure undergoing successive reincarnations throughout history. Like J-J Rousseau before him and D.H. Lawrence after him, Rimbaud toys with the idea that there was once a happy primitive state before mankind became emasculated by Christianity and perverted by Progress. In an earlier version of this translation I wrote, "Once upon a time, unless I am much mistaken, life [not *'my life'*] was a carnival where all hearts opened to one another..." but eventually I decided this was departing too far from the text.

p. 1   "I took Beauty upon my knees…"

At first sight Rimbaud's hostility to Beauty seems surprising. He presumably has in mind the idealised 'Beauty' of the late Romantic Parnassian movement — a movement to which he at first subscribed but soon rebelled against. Rimbaud had no time for the Art for Art's sake movement, which was just starting up at the time, because he was looking for a complete regeneration of humanity, not just a change of artistic fashion. In a rough sketch for *Une Saison en Enfer* we read *'l'art est une sottise'* — 'Art is rubbish'.

p. 1   "O poverty and hatred, my sorceresses, it was you who became the guardians of my treasure."

The sense is obscure but seems to be : 'Poverty and hatred, you were like sorceresses to me and helped me by guarding my treasure'.

   The 'guardians of the treasure' are perhaps the Rhinemaidens who appear in the opening scene of Wagner's *Rheingold* which was first staged in 1869 — four years before the publication of *Une Saison en Enfer* .
   'Sorcière' ('witch', 'sorceress') had a positive sense for Rimbaud who had probably just been reading Michelet's highly romanticised study of medieval witchcraft, *La Sorcière*, where witches are presented as rebels against Church and State and, in effect, as precursors of female emancipation.
   But what is the 'treasure' that they are guarding? Rimbaud's innocence? Or, again, his devastating insight into the true nature of the society in which he is born, in which case the allusion to the Ring of the Nibelung is most apt since Alberich has put a curse on the ring and it brings nothing but catastrophe to its possessors. But the treasure may be the mysterious *'Bonheur'* ('Happiness'?, 'Ecstasy'?) that holds a central place in Rimbaud's thinking — see the notes to the section *Délires II.*

p. 1 "....all hope for the future"

French: *'toute espérance humaine'* — lit. 'all human hope'. It is not clear whether this means 'all hope for the human species', or 'all the hope a human being can muster'. In any case, Rimbaud believes, or forces himself to believe, that there is no hope in either sense. (And yet apparently there is after all since Rimbaud eventually escapes from hell.)

p. 1 "...like a ravenous beast leaping upon its prey"

Rimbaud deliberately does not allow himself to partake of the normal pleasures of existence — he does not say why. The reason can only be, apart from his 'natural' masochistic tendencies, that the gruelling psycho-physical training Rimbaud believed to be essential for the aspiring poet/seer precluded his leading a comfortable life (see the fifth section of the chapter entitled *"Il a peut-être des secrets pour changer la vie?"* in *Rimbaud Revisited 1968 – 2008* where the famous Letter to Paul Demeny is discussed.)

p. 1 "Charity is the key"

The French *'charité'* has less unpleasant overtones than the English word — it is striking that there is no exact equivalent. *'Charité'* is a recurring theme in Rimbaud's writings and to a certain extent replaces *'amour'* in his world-view. Surprisingly, given what we know of Rimbaud's difficult character, Alfred Barley, Rimbaud's employer in Aden and Abyssinia, writes of his (Rimbaud's) *'charité, très discrète et large'* ('his discreet and considerable charitableness').

    Rimbaud is perhaps referring obliquely to the well-known passage in Saint Paul's *First Epistle to the Corinthians* which begins

> "Though I speak with the tongues of men and angels, and have not charity, I am become as sounding brass, or a tinkling cymbal..."

and concludes

> "And now abideth faith, hope, charity, these three; but the greatest of these is charity...."

Confronted with the intellectually brilliant Greek and Roman world of his time, St. Paul finds it wanting because it is lacking in 'charity', a virtue which the uneducated and despised Christians have in abundance. The original Greek word is *'agape'* and most modern translators render it as 'love'. But this has equally inappropriate Hollywood associations: St. Paul is speaking of the selfless communal love members of the Christian community have for one another regardless of age, looks and gender.

In much the same way, Rimbaud turns aside with disgust from the technologically advanced French society of his time because it has lost what is more important in his eyes. *'Charité'* is the key [to changing the world] because it is the behaviour which was current during the Golden Age and which in the degenerate modern era is practically non-existent since the members of bourgeois society Rimbaud sees around him are incapable of true generosity. However, in a typical *volte face* Rimbaud at once rules this out as any kind of a practical solution to the world's problems, for he goes on to say, "The very idea shows how far removed I was from reality". Why is such a suggestion deluded? Because a return to the earlier state of nature is impossible : Christianity and civilization mark a point of no return.

The idea of the return of a Golden Age when all things would be held in common and society would be bound together by universal love rather than fear, has a long history and can be traced at least as far back as Jewish and Early Christian Apocalyptic writings (see *The Pursuit of the Millennium*, by Norman Cohn). Although it is difficult to imagine this today, the very term 'communism' originally had highly romantic overtones : it conjured up the image of a society where everyone would be served according to their needs and the natural sources of wealth would be equitably shared out. In a rare description of what the future communist society would be like, the young Marx asks us to visualize people 'going off fishing in the morning and philosophizing in the afternoon' — as a French peasant friend of mine remarked, "Yes, nobody does any work".

p. 1 "...the following stark pages from the diary of a damned soul"

'Carnet d'un damné' (lit. 'Notebook of a damned man') is a very good description of *Une Saison en Enfer* and at one point I had thought of using it as the title of the translation : Rimbaud's text is the log-book kept by an explorer of an inner realm of darkness.

How seriously should one take this talk of being a 'damned soul'? It is certainly more than a passing Byronic pose, since Rimbaud returns to the theme several times. The third section *Nuit de l'Enfer* ('Hell-Fire') describes what it is like to actually be in hell and the one that follows it, *Délires I*, is supposed to be a direct communication from the infernal regions. However, from then on the theme of damnation becomes much less important than the theme of self-delusion to which it is not really related since damnation is a moral concept and self-delusion an intellectual one. Whereas Judeo-Christianity makes disobedience the cause of man's fall from grace, the 'Original Sin' in Buddhism, inasmuch as there is one, is 'misconception', 'misapprehension' which is remedied by 'correct perception', i.e. 'enlightenment'.

Rimbaud was brought up as a Catholic like practically everyone else in rural France at the time, and his mother was extremely devout. The extent to which this fatally influenced his thinking remains debatable — he himself at one point in the present work says "The marks of baptism are indelible" by which he presumably means that having once been initiated into the Christian mind-set one cannot ever completely throw it off. But Rimbaud's later life, in Abyssinia and elsewhere, though hardly carefree, does not look to me at all like the life of someone dogged by a sense of guilt in the manner of a Graham Greene hero. Rimbaud's sister, Isabelle, claimed that Rimbaud made a death-bed conversion. But she was an unreliable witness and in any case this matters little — it is how someone lives, not how he dies that is important.

We can take the feeling of 'damnation' as meaning that Rimbaud has had a momentary glimpse of paradise and then lost it —
"For this is hell, nor am I out of it.
Think'st thou that I who saw the face of God
And tasted the eternal joys of heaven,
Am not tormented by ten thousand hells,
In being deprived of everlasting bliss?"

as Mephistopheles puts it in Marlowe's *Doctor Faustus*.

Rimbaud's prose poem is the definitive modern statement of one of mankind's oldest and most tenacious myths, that of paradise lost. Rimbaud is acute enough to realize that the momentary apprehension of paradise in isolated mystic states, perhaps aided by drugs or magical procedures, is no sort of solution : on the contrary, it reinforces the sense of loss and estrangement — "for this [the normal world] is hell, nor am I out of it".

Strangely enough, so-called 'primitive' societies were themselves often preoccupied with the very same problem. "In the modern jargon, we might say that the (South American) savages regarded themselves, neither more nor less than if they had been Western Christians, as beings in a 'fallen' condition, by contrast with a fabulously happy situation in the past. Their actual condition was not their original one: it had been brought about by a catastrophe that had occurred *in illo tempore.* " (Mircea Eliade, *Myths, Dreams and Mysteries*)

The dilemma is essentially insoluble — or so it would appear.

p.2   Title : "PAGAN BLOOD"

French, *'Mauvais Sang'* (lit. 'Bad Blood'). Rimbaud originally planned a work entitled *Livre Païen* ('Pagan Book') of which this section is all that remains.

p. 2 "….I do not put butter in my hair"

Reputedly, the inhabitants of Gaul put butter in their hair much as the Romans used olive oil and ourselves gel.

p. 2 "…cattle-flayers and grass-burners"

Why grass-burners? Apparently, herdsmen used to burn the grass when it turned yellow ; a moving fire does not sterilise the earth and fresh grass would come up. Note that Rimbaud presents the Celts as herdsmen, not agriculturalists — despite identifying with the 'subject race' he never imagines himself as working on the land.

p. 2 "…the usual vices wrath, lecherousness – magnificent the latter!"

Mention of 'lecherousness' is more adolescent bravado than anything else. It seems unlikely that at this stage in his life Rimbaud had had many sexual relations with women, probably none at all. The nature of Rimbaud's sexuality is briefly discussed at the end of the chapter *"L'amour est à réinventer"* from *Rimbaud Revisited 1968 – 2008* in this volume.

p. 2 "I despise all occupations…"

Arthur Rimbaud's *lycée* in Charleville closed its gates in September 1870 because of the war with Prussia and Rimbaud never returned when it reopened. For the next two or three years he seems to have depended financially either on Verlaine or on his mother apart from giving a few French lessons in London. However, he subsequently became an interpreter in a travelling circus, foreman on a building-site in Cyprus, clerk in a commercial establishment in Aden and arms trafficker in Abyssinia to list only a few of his extraordinary — and by and large — thoroughly unsuccessful ventures. All in all, this makes a pretty laborious existence! Rather amusingly, considering this passage where the juvenile Rimbaud scorns the bourgeois work ethos, when his employer in Aden temporarily closed down his business he delivered to a certain Arthur Rimbaud the following certificate :

"14 Oct 1885

Je soussigné, Alfred Bardey, déclare avoir employé M. Arthur Rimbaud en qualité d'agent et d'acheteur depuis le 30 avril 1884 jusqu'en novembre 1885. Je n'ai qu'à me louer de ses services et de sa probité."

('I, Alfred Bardey, declare that I employed Mr. Arthur Rimbaud as representative and buyer for this firm between 30 April 1884 and November 1885. I was very satisfied indeed with his work and his honesty.')

p. 2 "Criminals disgust me like castrated bullocks: I am still intact and that's how I intend to remain."

French: *'Les criminels dégoûtent comme des châtrés : moi, je suis intact, et ça m'est égal'* — lit. 'Criminals are as disgusting as castrated persons: I am still intact and a good thing too'.

Why are criminals considered to be castrates? Presumably because the convict loses his freedom of action and thus access to females — but the sense is uncertain. In this passage, as in one or two others, Rimbaud states that he does not intend to take revolt so far as this. But more often he expresses great admiration for the criminal because he is defying bourgeois society.

p. 2 "Bourgeois and workers, baseborn fellows all."

French: "*Maîtres et ouvriers, tous paysans, ignobles*" — lit. 'Employers and workers, all peasants, ignoble lot'.
 The French *'paysan'* is virtually untranslatable since it is often applied to people we would simply call 'farmers'. In general, *'paysan'* does not have the pejorative sense of the English 'peasant' : a Frenchman today would probably use the word *'rustre'* to mean a 'crude person', or *'plouk'* if he wanted to be really insulting. But Rimbaud *does* mean the word as an insult : he didn't like *paysans* and lumped them together with the hated bourgeoisie.
 In gypsy parlance, as I came across it in the seventies when I lived in the South of France, *'paysan'* is used slightingly to refer to all sedentary persons whatever their trade or social station.

p. 2 "Families like my own…"

What exactly were Arthur Rimbaud's social origins? Arthur Rimbaud's father was a Captain in the Infantry who abandoned his wife and family and whom Arthur scarcely knew. Vitalie Rimbaud, the poet's mother, came from solid Ardenne landowning stock and she inherited a farm at Roche not far from Charleville where Rimbaud was brought up. She was not poor but she worked the land herself aided by her two daughters.
 Here, Rimbaud has in mind what we would call the middle classes — the French *'les classes moyennes'* is little used — people who rose to power with the French

Revolution which is why Rimbaud specifically mentions the Declaration of the Rights of Man.

p. 2 "I eat and drink with their elder sons."

French: *'J'ai connu chaque fils de famille'* — lit. 'I have known each son of [good] family'. The juvenile Rimbaud can hardly be said to have hobnobbed with high society : his main contacts in Charleville were a couple of French teachers who encouraged him to carry on writing and a slightly disreputable Inland Revenue Official who was interested in the occult. Rimbaud seems to be putting himself down for not being proletarian enough. Isabelle, Rimbaud's sister, recounts that her brother never took part in the *vendanges* and other agricultural tasks on the family farm, or at any rate not at this stage in his career — he does seem to have occasionally deigned to lend a hand later on when using Roche as a temporary base in between two trips to Africa or Java.

p. 3 "I swelled the numbers of the rabble marching to the Holy Land"

Apart from anything else, the Crusades proved to be a convenient means of getting rid of social misfits, rebels and impecunious younger sons. As he says, doubtless Rimbaud and many of his associates, likewise many Sixties hippies, would have been tempted had they been alive at the time : I remember an article in the popular French magazine *Actuel* in the seventies entitled, '*Un trip pas possible — la Guerre Sainte!*' ('For a really way out trip, try the Holy War').

p. 3 "I am dancing the witches' sabbath with old women and children"

Note no adult males present. Following the 19th century romantic historian Michelet, Rimbaud viewed medieval witches as exemplary social rebels and devotees of paganism.

Rimbaud does not seem to have actually practised magic, in the sense of casting spells and incantations, though he probably knew something of the writings of Éliphas Lévi and others from his Charleville friend, Bretagne. What he would have made of Wicca and the contemporary pagan revival I do not know. *Une Saison en Enfer* chronicles Rimbaud's ultimate disenchantment with both mystical and magical practices — both were incapable of transforming humanity.

p. 3 "And then, of course, we must not forget the pastimes of idle princes..."

Rimbaud means that many of today's sciences that are taken so seriously started off as hobbies and amusements for the aristocracy of the *siècle des lumières* : there is the story of Réaumur calling to his valet, "Bring in my laboratory, will you!"

p. 3 " Attention, folks, we are entering the Age of Mind..."

The French '*esprit*', most confusingly, means both 'spirit' and 'mind' and Rimbaud here plays on both meanings in a way that does not translate.
 The meaning seems to be this. Joachim de Fiore, an influential medieval mystic, divided history into three ages, that of the Father, the Son, and the Holy Spirit. The third and last age was to be one of universal peace and contentment. According to Rimbaud, the nineteenth century has replaced the old superstitions by apparently more sensible beliefs but really they are quite as unsatisfactory and chimerical as the previous ones. Instead of moving into the Age of the Spirit, in the sense of paradise regained, we are, so Rimbaud warns us, entering the Age of Mind marked by the one-sided development of Science, Rationalism and Democracy all of which Rimbaud totally despises at this stage in his life.

p. 4 "Alas! The Gospels have had their day…"

French : '*Hélas! L'Évangile a passé!*' — lit. 'Alas! the Gospel has passed!' i.e. 'has become out of date', is 'old hat'. Why have the Gospels become irrelevant to the modern world? Because the miraculous change announced by Christ in the Gospels has not taken place and never will now. The early Christians, including Saint Paul, expected Christ to return and wind up the historical process in their own lifetime. Rimbaud is not interested in theories or pious hopes but only in results and, as far as he is concerned, Christianity has not delivered the goods.

p. 4 "My day's work is ended. I am leaving Europe…"

Shortly after completing *Une Saison en Enfer*, Rimbaud did in fact embark on a number of extraordinary wanderings which took him as far afield as Aden, Java and Abyssinia. However, before finally settling in Harar, he made yearly trips back to the parental home at Charleville or Roche to recuperate before the next onslaught. It does not seem that, in his travels, Rimbaud ever came across a society leading the happy primitive life of which he dreamed : in this respect Gauguin in Tahiti was more successful.

p. 4 "Women go for these ferocious invalids returning from hot countries."

Curiously prophetic. On returning to France for treatment of a serious wound in 1891, Rimbaud had a leg amputated and was nursed for some months by his adoring sister, Isabelle, until his death at the end of the same year. Isabelle Rimbaud devoted much of the rest of her life to getting her brother's writings published; she was, however, a devout Catholic and seems to have deliberately withheld or suppressed certain documents.

p. 4 "What other lands? What other seas? The cross and the bayonet will surely follow me."

French: *'On ne part pas'* — lit. 'One does not leave' with the sense 'There is no escape'.
    I have allowed myself to add a phrase or two here but they are surely very Rimbaudian.

p. 4 "...my secret vice"

Presumably, masturbation, especially since he goes on to speak of it 'lifting [me] to the sky ' and then 'casting me down' (*'...qui monte au ciel, me bat, me renverse, me traîne'*). Some editors interpret the 'vice' as homosexuality but I find this implausible as I am far from convinced that Rimbaud really was homosexual.

p. 4 "Forward, the long march, the pack, boredom, fury".

During his bohemian existence in Paris, Brussels and London, Rimbaud was under perpetual threat of being called up for military service and this must have preyed on his mind. But when he returned from London to Charleville in December 1872 to sort out the situation, he was granted a reprieve because his brother had just enlisted in the regular army for five years.
    Rimbaud did enlist in the Dutch Colonial Army in 1876, three years after finishing *Une Saison en Enfer*, but he probably took this drastic step simply in order to get a free passage to the mysterious East. At any rate the experience does not seems to have appealed to him for he deserted three weeks after arriving in Java! On returning to Europe, Rimbaud offered his services the following year to the American Marines who wisely refused him, as did the Carlist forces fighting in Spain. Most biographers assume Rimbaud was after the bounty paid on enlistment. Verlaine also

attempted unsuccessfully to enlist in the Carlist volunteer army.
      One cannot see Rimbaud making a good soldier but we should forget the image of the provincial boy arriving in Paris with a satchel full of romantic poems to recite in literary cafés. The adult Rimbaud is described as being powerfully-built and broad-shouldered with prematurely white hair. He was for a while foreman on a building-site in Cyprus — which shows his employers considered him capable of exercising authority over navvies — and there is even a story that he killed a man accidentally in a fit of rage and fled to Alexandria to avoid being charged with manslaughter. It seems, however, that the story of Rimbaud actually being involved in the slave-trade is without foundation.

p. 5 "Think of my self-denial"

Presumably, sexual self-denial. If Rimbaud really had been homosexual, as many people claim, there would surely have been ample opportunities for a young, good-looking seventeen year old with no inhibitions on the loose in Paris. But getting hold of young women without paying them was another matter in the nineteenth century and it seems unlikely that Rimbaud frequented prostitutes at this period of his life — as Gauguin and Van Gogh, for example, did.

p. 5 "I idolised the hardened convict….."

Possibly Jean Valjean from *Les Misérables* by Victor Hugo which Rimbaud had certainly read. But Valjean was not a rebel against authority, nor was he sent overseas. Rimbaud had perhaps seen convicts passing through Charleville bound for the notorious French penal colony, Cayenne. Rimbaud's attitudes to criminals vary — a few lines back he referred to them as 'castrates'. But usually he admires them as supreme examples of rebellion against authority — a rebellion that, perversely, he considers to be all the more impressive because it lacks any underlying political or religious motivation .

p. 6 "a hundred million thunderbolts"

Reference to the Paris Commune which Rimbaud may have seen at close quarters. Delahaye claimed that Rimbaud volunteered to fight for the Free Forces and was even given some training at the barracks in Babylon, Paris. But it is unlikely that he actually fought, and most biographers agree that he was not in Paris during the *'semaine sanglante'*.

p. 6 "...handing me over to the authorities..."

Joan of Arc was tried for witchcraft (at the demand of the English whose captive she was) by an ecclesiastical court. Such courts did not have the right to impose the death penalty — like the Sanhedrin in the case of Christ — and, at the conclusion of the trial, they handed the guilty over to the temporal authorities 'with a recommendation towards mercy', though doubtless they made it clear what they wanted to be done. Contrary to what most people believe, Joan of Arc had to wait until the 20th century (1920) before she was officially canonised.

p. 6 "...the true kingdom of the progeny of Shem"

Shem, or Cham, was one of the sons of Noah (*Genesis 10. 1*) and reputedly the founder of the black race.

p. 7 "Divine love alone holds the key to knowledge"

i.e. 'divine love' rather than secular science and philosophy.

p. 7 "God is my strength and stay. Praise be to God."

It is not clear whether we are supposed to take this seriously or not — probably both at once. Such passages are an embarrassment to the many readers determined to view Rimbaud as an inveterate enemy of religion.

p.7 "Vice holds no appeal for me".

French: *"L'ennui n'est plus mon amour"* — lit. 'Tedium is no longer my love'.

Ennui is often translated as 'boredom' but has a much stronger and more corrosive sense. In Baudelaire's writings (which Rimbaud would have known) *ennui* signifies the overpowering sense of the futility of human existence, the world-weariness that the poet can only dispel by alcohol or opium, or by taking refuge in the arms of his beautiful mulatto mistress, Jeanne Duval.

This is certainly the sense here, since Rimbaud goes on to speak of *'les rages, la débauche et la folie'* — states brought on by *ennui* and which Rimbaud no longer indulges in. Pascal also says in his *Pensées* that most human crimes and folly are provoked by the same sentiment of chronic tedium and dissatisfaction, but, for Pascal, only a sense of the proximity and love of God was an effective antidote.

p. 8 "I do not regret the century of breviaries and preciosity"

French: *"Je ne regrette pas le siècle des cœurs sensibles"* — lit. 'I do not regret the century of sensitive hearts' or 'I do not regret the century of sensibility'. Some editors take this as referring to the 18th century, but surely the 17th century is more appropriate. During the time of Louis XIV it was fashionable to parade extravagant sentiments, and Molière satirises these sorts of people in *Les Précieuses Ridicules*. The 18th century was *le siècle des lumières*.

p. 8 "....action, the focal point of the present world"

French: *"ma vie n'est pas assez pesante, elle s'envole et flotte loin au-dessus de l'action, ce cher point du monde"* — lit. 'my life is not heavy enough, it takes off and floats high above action, that beloved point of the world'.

Rimbaud seems to be mixing his metaphors here. The first part I take to be a reference to ballooning : the idea is that Rimbaud's life lacks the necessary ballast to keep it down to earth, i.e. concerned with mundane things like looking for a job and getting married. Most editors take *'ce cher point du monde'* as an oblique reference to Archimedes's remark, "Give me a fixed point and I will move the world". However, it doesn't make a lot of sense to be floating above a 'fixed point'. The general sense though is clear : Rimbaud views himself as temperamentally incapable of making any active contribution to the society of his time. *'Travail, Famille, Patrie'* was not for him.

p. 10 Title : "HELL-FIRE"

French: *'Nuit d'Enfer'* — lit. 'Night in Hell'. In an earlier version, Rimbaud entitled this section *'Fausse Conversion'* ('False Conversion').

p. 10 "...a fantastic mouthful of poison"

The poison is clearly moral, not physical. But what exactly? Guilt due to his Christian upbringing? Self-doubt? Loss of nerve?

All things considered, I think the 'poison' is Rimbaud's previous inflated idea of himself as magician/poet which, in the light of experience, he realises is not an effective way to change humanity or even himself. This is why, in this section, he writes that 'hallucinations are endless' and caricatures himself as a fairground conjuror or 19th century adman.

p. 10 "Someone who wants to mutilate himself is indeed a damned soul, is he not?"

Was Rimbaud masochistic in the literal sense? He speaks in more than one place of self-mutilation (see *Délires I*) but we should distinguish between inflicting pain on oneself and wanting to be beaten or maltreated by someone else for sexual pleasure. Rimbaud clearly had a very strong self-punishing streak in his character but he was usually dominant, not to say overbearing, in his dealings with other people — his treatment of Verlaine is not far from being sadistic.

p. 10   "A crime, quick, so the depths will yawn and swallow me up for good and proper".

French: *'Un crime, vite, que je tombe à néant, de par la loi humaine'* — lit. 'A crime, quick, so I can collapse into nothingness, as human law would have it.'
    I take it that what Rimbaud means is that he would rather be well and truly damned but that, as yet, he hasn't done anything bad enough. *'De par la loi humaine'* presumably means 'as by rights I should be' but the meaning is unclear.

p. 11   *'moonlight when the village clock strikes twelve'*....

 French: *'le clair de lune quand le clocher sonnait douze'*. The phrase is in italics in the original edition of 1873 which Rimbaud himself had checked, so it is most likely a quotation from a poem, perhaps written by Verlaine. But no one as yet has tracked it down.

p. 11 "...no faith in the historical process..."

French: *'plus de foi en l'histoire'* — lit. 'no more faith in history'.
  As against nineteenth century progressive thinkers, Rimbaud denies that history is leading us anywhere worthwhile.

p. 11 "Ferdinand"

Apparently a nickname of the Devil in the Ardennes. Exactly why he is running off with the 'wild seeds' is unclear : Rimbaud is perhaps recalling some well-known print or illustration in a children's book. Some editors take *'les graines sauvages'* in the sense of 'bad boys', 'dissolute persons' — in English we have the expression 'a bad seed'.

p. 11 "My lantern reveals his features to me."

Probably 'magic lantern' which was very popular with families at the time. The title of Rimbaud's other principal prose work, *Les Illuminations*, most likely refers to images projected from a magic lantern.

p. 11 "I shall now unveil a series of mysteries...."

Rimbaud is satirising himself by mimicking the patter of the fairground magician mixed in with overtones of the revivalist preacher. The message once again is that his (Rimbaud's) earlier faith in 'magic' and the 'poetic imagination' is no more worthy to be taken seriously than the preposterous claims of wandering conjurors. On the other hand, the passage reads so well one wants to be taken in!

p. 12 "to the sick tossing in their hospital beds, and to our dark brethren overseas…"

The French merely says, *'Pauvres, travailleurs'* — 'the poor and the workers', but my addition is surely in the spirit of the passage!

p. 13 Title : "DELIRIUM 1 Dramatis Personae Foolish Virgin Infernal Bridegroom"

The French just says *'Délires I Vierge Folle L'Époux Infernal'*.

Although some editors, see fit to deny it, *Délires 1,* is surely based on Rimbaud's tempestuous relation with the French poet, Verlaine (see *Rimbaud Revisited).* In a sense, it does not really matter since the two opposed characters are presented as archetypes (or stereotypes).

The **Parable of the Wise and Foolish Virgins** is given in **Matthew 25 vv. 1-13**. The five Foolish Virgins are to meet the Bridegroom with lamps but they have forgotten to bring any oil. When the Bridegroom arrives unexpectedly the Foolish Virgins try to borrow some oil from the five Wise Virgins who refuse, saying there will not be enough to go round if they do this. The five Foolish Virgins go into the town to try and buy some oil.

> "**10** And while they went to buy, the bridegroom came; and they that were ready went in with him to the marriage; and the door was shut.
> **11** Afterward came also the other virgins, saying, Lord, Lord, open to us.
> **12** But he answered and said, Verily I say unto you, I know ye not."

The moral is that the Foolish Virgins have 'missed the boat' and entirely by their own fault — a surprisingly harsh message to find in the New Testament.

Like the Foolish Virgins waiting for the Marriage Feast, which in the Gospel story symbolises eternal life in paradise, the widow is not prepared for the imminent apocalyptic event which, in the Rimbaudian scheme, will lead to the regeneration of humanity, to the *'ancien festin retrouvé'*. Rimbaud himself has broken once and for all with the bonds of Christianity, family and conventional morality which is why he casually identifies himself with the Infernal Bridegroom. But the widow (Verlaine) is pulled both ways at once: she is fascinated by the idea of personal emancipation that Rimbaud represents in her eyes but is always backsliding into conventional piety, having it both ways at once, or trying to.

p.17 "the assumption of my little friend"

The 'assumption' of the widow's 'little friend' is an ironic travesty of the Assumption of the Holy Virgin taken up to Heaven by angels. But the speaker is not being sarcastic. She sees her 'little friend' as frightening but also as someone altogether different from other people, endowed with supernatural abilities : *'Je me réveillerai, et les lois et les mœurs auront change — grâce à son pouvoir magique'* ('I shall wake up one day to find that the laws and customs of humanity have all changed, thanks to his magic power').

p. 18 "Now me."

Having settled his account with the Verlaine type of inhabitant of Hell, Rimbaud turns to himself and is just as merciless. If Verlaine is in Hell for self-pity and indecision, Rimbaud is in Hell for delusion. Each to his own.

p. 18 "I adored bric-à-brac....."

French: *'les peintures idiotes'* — lit. 'silly paintings'. In the list of things Rimbaud approves of I have given what I consider to be the nearest equivalents rather than literal translations.

Rimbaud likes the very objects that 'true artists' of the time looked down on. But this is not Dada or contemporary 'Conceptual Art': the things Rimbaud shows affection for are all genuine and above all *unpretentious*. Rimbaud would have had nothing but contempt for 'anti-art' that insists on being treated as art.

p. 18   "I dreamed crusades, Antarctic expeditions lost with all hands, short-lived republics, mystical movements stamped out by the sword…"

French: *'Je rêvais croisades, voyages de découvertes dont on n'a pas de relations, républiques sans histories, guerres de religion étouffées'* — lit. 'I dreamed crusades, voyages of discovery that left no records, republics without a history, suppressed wars of religion'.

p. 18   "I invented the colour of vowels!"

A ridiculous amount of critical acumen has been devoted to this claim of Rimbaud's, which is developed at greater length in his poem *Voyelles* ('Vowels') written some two years earlier.
   Synesthesia, is "the production of a mental sense-impression relating to one sense by the stimulation of another sense" (Concise Oxford Dictionary). The experience of synesthesia is not that rare: about one person in every two thousand is afflicted (or graced) with it according to Chris Frith (*Making up the Mind*, Blackwell, 2007). Synesthetes typically associate a letter of the alphabet with a colour or shape. They by no means always agree about the 'colour' of letters of the alphabet: the Russian novelist Nabokov claimed to 'see' the letter M as pink, while his wife saw it as blue. We are perhaps all synesthetes in a mild way since we readily speak of 'warm colours' or 'sharp sounds' (or tastes) without the slightest sense of incongruity.
   Rimbaud may have been a synesthete to some degree (as I was myself as an adolescent) but he goes a good deal

further since, a few lines later, he speaks of inventing "a new poetical language which, once perfected, would affect all the five senses simultaneously". This would be magic indeed and would justify the extravagantly high opinion the adolescent Rimbaud had of the power of the spoken, or written, word. In a sense Rimbaud's 'new poetical language' already exists : it is contemporary 'virtual reality'.

pp. 19 - 23 Rimbaud seems to be recalling the poems in this section from memory since they are not always identical with other versions.

p. 19   "Liquid gold that took my sense away"

Reference to alchemy in which Rimbaud was interested for a while.

p. 20   "How long must I wait for it, how long, The Time of my Heart's Desire?"

French: *'Qu'il vienne, qu'il vienne/Le temps dont on s'éprenne'* — lit. 'May it come, may it come, the time one is in love with'. In a manuscript version of the poem we have

> *"Ah! Que le temps vienne*
> *Où les cœurs s'éprennent!"*

which is quite different, meaning 'If only the time would come when hearts fall in love!' This version of the refrain is preferable both in terms of rhythm and sense.

p. 21 'General, if you have only so much as a single rusty cannon on your ruined ramparts, bombard us with blocks of dried earth.

Direct your fire at the fashionable boutiques and salons!'

Reference once again to the Commune. Rimbaud is imploring the besiegers to destroy the symbols of bourgeois wealth, boutiques and salons.

**p. 21 "I have found her, have found her —
 Who? — Eternity.
 She is the rays of the sun
 Falling across the sea."**

I take this as meaning that the 'eternal' is to be found in the instant: in simple things like the pattern of light on water. This is the essential message of Zen — or that part of it that is genuine and valuable.

p. 23 "Once I even fell in love with a pig."

Some editors take this as a slighting reference to Verlaine who had a good-living side to him.

p. 23 "Cimmeria, land of whirlpools and enigmas"

For the Greeks, Cimmeria was a land of mist and cloud at the very confines of the known world. Ulysses touches down here before descending into the Underworld.

p. 23 "....I loved the ocean as if it had the power to wash away my sins"

'Sins' is possibly too strong : the French is *'souillure'* — lit. 'stain', 'blemish'. But the term is frequently used in a religious context, and in the same sentence there is mention of *'la croix consolatrice'*.

p. 23 "I was damned by the rainbow".

French: *'J'avais été damné par l'arc-en-ciel'* — lit. 'I had been damned by the rainbow'. Haunting phrase that has been variously interpreted.
   Rimbaud has just been talking about the ocean 'washing away his sins' (or 'stains') In **Genesis 9 vv. 8-17** the rainbow is presented as the sign of God's forgiveness of mankind after destroying the greater part of the human race in the Flood. It is intended to be a reminder, to mankind and to God Himself, that such a calamity shall never come to pass again:

> "**13** I do set my bow in the cloud, and it shall be for a token of a covenant between me and the earth. (…)
> **15** And I will remember my covenant, which is between me and you and every living creature of all flesh : and the waters shall no more become a flood to destroy the earth."

Many editors think that Rimbaud is 'damned by the rainbow' because he believes, or chooses to believe, that he is not included in the general pardon. But then, he would probably not have wanted to be involved in it anyway, preferring to go his own way and run the risk of a second Flood, rather than kowtowing to the Almighty like Noah and his sons (who are not sympathetic figures). Rimbaud's need for absolution remains, however. The chief drawback of pantheism as a religion is that Nature is totally indifferent to man and so there is no hope of being 'saved' or 'forgiven' by Nature: man must either do this by himself, or not at all.
   But this by no means exhausts the possible meaning of the phrase. There is also surely the sense that the rainbow as a thing of beauty, precisely *because* it is so beautiful, is dangerous, life-threatening. Rimbaud's rainbow is *La Belle Dame Sans Merci* of Keats's poem or Housman's 'heartless,

witless' but sublimely beautiful Nature 'that neither cares nor knows'.

Rimbaud's contradictory — but perfectly comprehensible — attitudes call to mind those of the main character in Yukio Mishima's novel *The Temple of the Golden Pavilion*. The protagonist is, from a very early age, obsessed with the famous temple Kinkakukji, eventually lives as a monk inside it and at one stage expects to be put in charge of it on the death of the current master. But he finds that Kinkakuji, as a symbol of transcendent beauty, always intervencs as a barrier between himself and ordinary life : to use a fairly crude example of its fatal attraction, it rises before his eyes every time he is with a girl and makes him impotent. In the end, the protagonist, much like Rimbaud who 'turns Beauty away with insults' at the very beginning of *Une Saison en Enfer*, burns the temple to the ground. This powerful though unhealthy novel is based on a real incident: a young Zen monk, who said during his trial that he "hated his own ugly, stammering self", deliberately set fire to the Temple of the Golden Pavilion, regarded as one of the most beautiful Buddhist shrines in the whole of Japan. (It has been rebuilt, incidentally, and some say the new one is even more beautiful than the old.)

p. 24 "Ecstasy was my fatality, my remorse, my curse...."

French: *'Le Bonheur était ma fatalité, mon remords, mon ver'* — lit. 'Happiness was my fatality, my remorse, my curse'. 'Happiness' seems too weak : in any case the French *bonheur* has a stronger sense than the bland English 'happiness' and Rimbaud (who checked the proofs of *Une Saison en Enfer*) has *'Bonheur'* with capital *B*. In this and other passages Rimbaud contrasts *'Bonheur'* with *'beauté'* (no capital letter) entirely to the advantage of the former — in the previous line he has stated that his life had always seemed to him *'trop immense pour être dévouée à la force et à la beauté'* — lit. 'too immense to be devoted entirely to strength and beauty'.

One is sometimes tempted to view Rimbaud's *'Bonheur'* as simply 'orgasm' but this seems too simplistic. To equate *Bonheur* with 'grace' (in the sense of 'Amazing Grace') would be going too far in the opposite direction though once again there may be a suggestion of this. *Bonheur* perhaps signifies 'peace of mind', *ataraxia,* the aim of both the ancient Stoic and Epicurean philosophies. A little further on Rimbaud speaks of *'la magique étude du bonheur'* — lit. the 'magic study of happiness' — which has an alchemical feel to it.

At the same time, *'Bonheur'* is apparently tied to Rimbaud's personal life in the here and now since in the last two lines of the poem Rimbaud says that

"L'heure de sa fuite, hélas!
Sera l'heure du trépas."

lit. 'the hour of its flight, will be the hour of [my] death'.

This couplet suggests yet other interpretations, the Spiritualists' 'astral body' which is supposedly connected to the physical body by a silver cord : if this cord is severed physical death results.

p. 24 "... warned me at the crowing of the cock — *ad matutinem*, at the *Christus venit* — in the most desolate of towns....

Matins is not necessarily a morning office which is presumably why Rimbaud adds the Latin phrase *'ad matutinem'* — 'in the morning'. Morning matins, which is traditionally recited just before daybreak, is followed by lauds and Steinmetz usefully points out that Sunday lauds contains the verse *'Gallo canente spes redit'* — 'Hope returns with the crowing of the cock'. Rimbaud, who was a good Latinist, would have been familiar with this verse from his Catholic upbringing.

In folk tales it is the crowing of the cock that summons wandering spirits back to their place in the Underworld. There may be something of this sense in the allusion as well.

p. 24 "I now know how to greet beauty."

Rimbaud unexpectedly ends this section by affirming that, after all, he now knows how to 'greet' beauty which at the beginning of *Une Saison en Enfer* he had 'driven away with insults'.

p. 25   Title : "UTOPIA"

French *"L'Impossible"* — lit. 'the impossible'. I had thought of using 'Eden' as the title. In any case, the sense is clear: the dream of the return of the Earthly Paradise is doomed, it is 'impossible'.

This section is crucial if one wants to grasp the development of Rimbaud's thought. Rimbaud now realises that the situation is more complicated than he had originally thought: it is not simply a matter of sloughing off the Christian sense of guilt and refusing to be a dupe of progress. The rot goes deeper still and the 'original sin' turns out to be intellectual rather than moral or psychological: it has something to do with Western habits of thought, worrying what life is about "instead of just living". This is precisely the message of Zen: the ultimate wisdom is to see and take things as they are.

The final note struck is sombre — the last line is *Déchirante infortune!* — but, surprisingly, from this point onwards the tone picks up considerably and the 'Journal of a Damned Soul' ends on a note of muted triumph. Why is this? Has Rimbaud acquired some special new insight? Only the 'insight' that the whole business (looking for the meaning of life, soul-searching, considering oneself to be a damned soul, wanting to be saved, &c. &c.) is just a waste of time and energy. The solution, then, is that there is and can be no solution because there should never have been any problem. QED.

p. 25 "That life I used to lead..."

Rimbaud dismisses the vagrant life he had been leading on and off during the preceding two or three years as pointless because he now sees that it is neither a personal nor a general solution to mankind's troubles. Some hundred years or so before the hippie movement got going with its motto of *'Tune In, Turn On and Drop Out'*, Rimbaud went through the self-same changes, rejecting family life, education, refusing to work, sleeping rough, defying sexual taboos, smoking hashish, and so on.

From now on Rimbaud will continue travelling — he will go much further afield — but he will be on the look out for well-paid employment and, like so many others of his time, will try to make his pile in the colonies before returning to the home country. In one of his letters to his mother from Harar he even goes so far as to say he regrets not being married and having a family (*'Pour moi, je regrette de ne pas être marié et avoir une famille'*)! The bohemian life is over for good.

p. 25 "And yet I was surely right to despise those pathetic idiots who will do anything to get their hands on a female...."

This is perhaps a reference to Verlaine who kept on returning to the marital fold until his wife decided that enough was enough. There is, of course, an inherent contradiction in Rimbaud's attitudes to sex and women — but this is typical of most, if not all, male advocates of sexual liberation. On the one hand, especially in his early poems, Rimbaud is an out and out advocate of complete sexual freedom at a time when marriage and a pretence at fidelity were still *de rigueur*, even in artistic circles. But at the same time Rimbaud is obviously terrified of being trapped into domesticity — and says as much at several points in *Une Saison en Enfer*. It is rather absurd that editors and critics invariably take Rimbaud's side in the Verlaine affair and even criticise Verlaine's long-suffering wife : I don't know how she was supposed to react to an arrogant, penniless seventeen year old going off with her husband and to boot lecturing him about 'being bourgeois' because he periodically felt some responsibility for his wife and children.

p. 25 " particularly in these days when there is such disaccord between us".

I was tempted to write "particularly in these days when there is so much talk of emancipation", but in the end decided that this would be reading contemporary concerns back into the past. There must have been some talk about equal rights for women amongst the French political émigrés that Verlaine and Rimbaud frequented for a while in London. But, despite Louise Michel and other famous figures, Women's Lib seems to have made slow progress in France — the French Socialist Party for a long time opposed votes for women — and I was amazed (and repulsed) by the crude macho style still acceptable in political magazines as late as the Sixties even amongst hyper-advanced groups like the *Internationale Situationniste*. (The usual idea was to associate revolutionary vigour with the ability to give young girls fantastic orgasms.) During May 1968 not a single woman emerged as a prominent figure and French feminists subsequently claimed that their posters were ripped down by so-called 'revolutionaries' in the Sorbonne (see the author's reminiscences *Le Temps des Cérises: May '68 and Aftermaths* in **The Raven Anarchist Quarterly 38** published by Freedom Press).

p. 25 "since I am putting all that behind me".

Because Rimbaud has already decided to leave Europe, though he may also mean that he is putting all this bohemian life in Paris behind him, including (probably non-existent) relations with women.

p. 25 "We shake hands, pass the time of day, but at bottom we feel nothing but disgust for one another."

The 'they' are presumably Rimbaud's bohemian Paris friends with most of whom he has by now quarrelled.

p. 25 "But what about the better type of person, the elite?"

French: *'élus'* which, annoyingly, has on the one hand the Calvinistic sense of 'the elect' but also the civic sense 'elected officials'. In any case, Rimbaud detests both types so it doesn't really matter.

This is an obscure passage. Rimbaud seems to be saying that those who pass for being a 'better type of person' are just hypocrites. There are, he concedes, certain 'embittered, joyous fellows' who are 'the true élite' inasmuch as there is one — but he adds a warning, *'Ce ne sont pas des bénisseurs!'* — lit. 'they're not people who give you a blessing!', i.e. they are a pretty rough lot.

p. 26 "Mind is stronger than matter, and my mind tells me that I am an inhabitant of the West whether I like it or not."

French: *'Les philosophes: Le monde n'a pas d'âge'* — lit. 'Philosophers will tell you that the world has no special age'.

Highly condensed passage. I take it Rimbaud is ridiculing the self-satisfied philosophers who claim that there are no 'ages of humanity', since 'thought is timeless'.

p. 26   "I return to the East....."

The latter nineteenth century saw a greatly increased interest in Indian and Chinese literature and philosophy. But the East for Rimbaud includes the Middle East, or at any rate parts of it. It is accepted today that the 'fertile crescent' was the cradle of civilization since it was in Mesopotamia that writing and arithmetic were first developed. The Garden of Eden was supposedly situated 'in the East' and the Magi — 'Wise Men' rather than kings — came from 'the East', i.e. Persia. Rimbaud would like to think that there was an 'original wisdom' which has since been obscured by Westerners. In a sense he was quite right, since many historians today see ethical dualism (Light/Dark, Good/Evil, God/Satan etc.) as originating in the Middle East (modern Iran/Iraq) and having found classic expression in Zoroastrianism which in turn had a considerable influence on Jewish and Early Christian thought, e.g. the idea that the cosmos and the microcosm, the human individual within it, were a perpetual battleground for the opposing forces of Good and Evil. But Rimbaud would hardly have approved of such notions. Much of what he views as 'Western' turns out to have been imported from the Middle East, the birth-place of three out of the five main world religions, Judaism, Christianity and Islam (the other two being Buddhism and Hinduism).

p. 26   "...the bastard wisdom of the Koran".

A 'bastard wisdom' because, although originating in Arabia, Islam contains many Judeo-Christian borrowings — which Rimbaud insists on viewing as 'Western'. To obtain a 'pure' ancient wisdom more to his taste, Rimbaud would have been obliged to make the trip to Katmandu or Benares.

p. 26 "....that world-famous declaration of scientific principles, Christianity..."

We are more used to seeing Christianity attacked as superstition compared to the sober truths of science and rationalism. But Christianity is already too questioning, too intellectual for Rimbaud's taste and thus all of a piece with the modern sceptical, scientific mentality that Rimbaud hates. Certainly, Christianity and science agree in totally rejecting instinct and intuition.

p. 26 "It [the original wisdom] would seem to be a gospel of unadulterated idleness!"

Rimbaud is most likely thinking of the *Tao Te Ching* which praises 'Not-Doing' as against 'Doing'.

p. 26 "humanity has been playing a game with itself, has found it necessary to prove the obvious, is pathetically fond of repeating over and over these very same proofs — and has forgotten how to live in any other way!

Exactly the message of Zen though Rimbaud probably didn't know this.

p. 26 "M. Prudhomme comes from the same stable as Christ."

M. Prudhomme, the epitome of the pompous, self-satisfied bourgeois, was a character invented by the writer Henri Monnier.
   Examples of statements attributed to M. Prudhomme are:
   "C'est mon opinion et je la partage." ('That's my opinion, and I heartily agree with it.')
   "Ôtez l'homme de la société, vous l'isolez." ('Take a man away from society, and you isolate him.')

> *"Napoleon 1er était un ambitieux; s'il avait voulu rester simple officier d'artillerie, il serait peut-être encore sur le trône."* ('Napoleon was an ambitious fellow; if he had been content to remain a simple artillery officer, he might well still be on the throne.')

But why should M. Prudhomme resemble Christ? For Rimbaud there is something hopelessly pedestrian about God getting himself incarnated as a 'human being' to 'prove' to people that he (God) exists and cares for them — from the standpoint of the 'original wisdom' there would be no need for proofs.

p. 27 "…nothing to be gleaned from the early history of China and Japan"

The text does not mention China and Japan specifically, only *'peuples orientaux'*.

p. 27 "And what relevance has the purity of bygone times to my own dream for the future?

This is the crux of the matter. History is not cyclic and once paradise is lost, it is lost for ever. Who cares what people were like thousands of years ago?

p. 27 "Peoples move about….."

Passing reference to what was at the time a novel theory, that the earth's peoples had not always been native to a particular spot but had moved about across the globe.

p. 27 "Desperate and hopeless humanity!

French: *'Déchirante infortune!'* — lit. 'heart-rending misfortune!'

p. 28 " 'Nothing is vanity! Believe in science and forward march!' cries the modern Ecclesiastes"

Rimbaud means that his own era of 'progress' believes it has exactly reversed the message of the author of *Ecclesiastes* :

> "**2** Vanity of vanities, saith the Preacher, vanity of vanities; all is vanity.
> **3** What profit hath a man of all his labour which he taketh under the sun?
> **4** One generation passeth away, and another generation cometh...
> **9** The thing that hath been, it is that which shall be; and that which is done is that which shall be done: and there is no new thing under the sun."

But the latter 19th century, intoxicated with its technological and scientific achievements, considers that humanity is really getting somewhere at last and that the Golden Age is just round the corner.

Rimbaud begs to differ. Just as the author of *Ecclesiastes*, a cultivated Jew of the Hellenistic era, denies that there is, or can be, anything really new, Rimbaud, the brilliant 19th century *lycéen* who carried off the prizes for Latin and French composition at school, dismisses science and philosophy in 'Pagan Blood' as the same old stuff dressed up in different language. There are in fact several close parallels between these two literary masterpieces separated by some two thousand years, for the author of *Ecclesiastes* has clearly just gone through an agonising psychological and religious crisis very similar to Rimbaud's. Like Rimbaud, he ends up by turning against his own tortured intellectualism — "Of making books there is no end; and much study is a weariness of the flesh". The world-weary Jewish philosopher does, however, manage to strike a final note of resignation to the Will of God (or, if you like, to Nature), a note which by and large is absent from *Une Saison en Enfer* though there are (ironical?) flashes of it here and there, for example, *"Le monde est bon. Je bénirai la vie. J'aimerai mes frères. Ce ne sont pas des promesses d'enfance. (...) Dieu fait ma force, et je loue Dieu."* which I have translated

> "The world is good. In my last moments, I shall bless the gift of life, love all men as brothers. This is no mere New Year's resolution. (...) God is my strength and stay, praise be to God." (p. 5)

'Preacher' is a somewhat misleading translation of the Hebrew *Koheleth* since it conjures up the image of an open-air evangelist which the sombre and retiring author of *Ecclesiastes* most certainly was not. The term can also mean 'someone who collects wise sayings for the purpose of teaching' (*Dictionary of the Bible*), i.e. what used to be called a 'moralist'. The first verse of the Old Testament book attributes authorship to the 'Son of David', i.e. King Solomon, but this is just convention. There seems general agreement today that *Ecclesiastes* was written by a wealthy, cultured Jew living in the early 2nd century BC.

p. 28 "my self-betrayal [would be] too brief an agony"

French: *'ma trahison au monde serait un supplice trop court'* — lit. 'my betrayal to the world would be too brief a torture'. I had thought of writing 'selling out' for *'trahison'* : this is how I interpret the sentence anyway. But Steinmetz (*Rimbaud*, Flammarion) takes *'trahison au monde'* in the opposite sense, as a 'defection', 'refusal of duty', i.e. Rimbaud has not done what is expected of him by society.

p. 28 "....eternity would be well and truly lost to us, would it not?"

Eternal bliss would be 'well and truly lost' because Rimbaud would not have led the required life of duty and hard work and at the last moment would have 'lashed out in all directions'.
 Once again, it is not clear whether Rimbaud is being ironic or not.

p. 29 "...the Biblical hell, whose gates were once opened by the Son of Man".

Christ, as the Apostles' Creed reminds us, did not go straight up to Heaven after his death — *"And He descended into Hell, and on the third day He rose again"*. The Last Judgement was a Persian idea which the Jews only picked up during the Babylonian Captivity. According to the oldest Jewish tradition everyone, high or low, good or bad, went to Sheol, so Christ was, as it were, completing his incarnation. But after Christ's brief visit everything changed, at least in the eyes of Christians: for Christ threw open the 'gates of Hell', thus allowing certain individuals (the just) to move up to Heaven, or so certain traditions would have it. This is the 'Harrowing of Hell' as the Authorised version puts it in a graphic phrase. In *Revelation* there is an interval of a thousand years — hence the term 'millennium' — before the final overthrow of the Devil and the complete destruction of Hell along with all the wicked.
 Like Christ, Rimbaud has 'opened the gates of Hell', i.e. glimpsed what it is like to live there, but at present he is preparing to move on, literally since he is 'leaving Europe for good', and conceptually, because he has finished with all this pointless soul-searching.

p. 29 "the three kings — the heart, the mind and the soul"

Rimbaud continues to parallel (not parody) the Christian message. Instead of awaiting the birth of an otherworldly Saviour, Rimbaud expects and hopes for the coming of a 'new order' in the here and now, a 'new idea of work', the end of tyranny and superstition, and so forth. The awaited Messiah is not an otherworldly Saviour but simply a regenerated humanity. The 'three kings' are no longer 'Wise Men from the East' but, in this strictly humanistic interpretation, they represent the three constituents of the human being, the heart, the soul and the spirit (this division of the human being was made by certain neo-Platonists).

Quite unexpectedly, in this penultimate section, Rimbaud writes what someone described as a 'moving hymn of revolutionary aspiration'.

p. 30 Title : "SILENCE AND EXILE"

French: '*Adieu*'. The title in my translation refers to the last line of James Joyce's *Portrait of the Artist as a Young Man* when the author says farewell to Ireland and sums up his plans for his future life as "Silence, exile and cunning."

p. 30 "The sinister Queen"

Rimbaud is simultaneously alluding to Queen Victoria and to Proserpine, the Queen of the Underworld, which is why he goes on to speak of the "*millions d'âmes et de corps morts et qui seront jugés*" ('millions of souls and dead bodies who are awaiting judgment') since Proserpine and Dis judged human beings after their death.

Victorian London is equated to Hell — the City of Eternal Night of Francis Thompson, the 'port of suffering' where Rimbaud and Verlaine lived on and off during the period 1872-3...

p. 30 "the unidentified bodies…"

This time Rimbaud is referring to Paris after the defeat of the Commune in May 1871 and the summary executions during the *semaine sanglante* (May 21-8 1871). Rimbaud, in his highly condensed manner, is combining personal impressions of the two capitals, London and Paris. Rimbaud may have witnessed the execution scenes himself though most of his biographers think this is unlikely.

p. 31 " suicides — degenerates from a bygone era".

French: *'amis de la mort'* — lit. 'death-lovers'.
    I was tempted to write 'suicide bombers' and this is certainly the sense. Rimbaud means that he no longer feels jealous (as he once did) of persons who were more socially unacceptable than he was himself, for example criminals, down-and-outs, suicides.

p. 31 "nothing behind me but that hideous stunted tree"

French: *'arbrisseau'* — lit. 'shrub'. Some people have seen this as an ironic allusion to the Burning Bush of Moses, but this seems fanciful to me.

p. 31 "I have witnessed the degradation of women down here and soon it will be permitted me to hold in my arms the truth in a soul and a body."

Rimbaud concludes the account of his 'season in Hell' with a typically nineteenth century expression of romantic love, or desire for it. When I did the first draft of this translation many years ago I viewed *Une Saison en Enfer* as a manifesto in favour of the life of the senses, sexual freedom and the liberation of women. These are certainly recurring themes but in retrospect seem less crucial than other issues such as the transformation of humanity and the intellectual and moral sickness of the West. However, it is on the note of *'L'amour est à réinventer'* that Rimbaud decides to end his great work, so maybe he should be classed with the Romantics after all.

(April – August 2008)

Rimbaud Revisited
1968 — 2008

"Il a peut-être des secrets pour changer la vie?"

(Délires I)

WHEN I made the first draft of this translation of *Une Saison en Enfer* in the early Seventies, I viewed Rimbaud essentially as a pantheist and rabid opponent of Christianity. There's certainly plenty of evidence for such an interpretation of Rimbaud though not so much as I imagined if we stick strictly to *Une Saison en Enfer* : the real *pièces à conviction* for such a viewpoint are early poems such as 'Les Premières Communions' and 'Soleil et Chair'.

> *"— O Vénus, ô Déesse !*
> *Je regrette le temps de l'antique jeunesse*
> *Des satyrs lascifs, des faunes animaux…*
> *Je crois en toi ! je crois en toi ! Divine mere,*
> *Aphrodite marine ! — Oh ! la route est amère*
> *Depuis que l'autre Dieu nous attelle à sa croix;*
> *Chair, Marbre, Fleur, Vénus, c'est en toi que je crois !"*

> "O Venus! Goddess! How I regret that ancient youthful era peopled by lustful satyrs and fauns… I believe in you! I believe in you! Divine mother, Aphrodite who rose from the sea! How bitter the path is since the other god yoked us to his cross; Flesh, Marble, Flower, Venus, it is in you that I believe!"

This is certainly where Rimbaud was coming from but by 1872-3 he no longer quite subscribed to such a simple pantheistic faith though there are echoes of it here and there especially in the section *Mauvais Sang* ('Pagan Blood').

Re-reading *Une Saison en Enfer* today, I see it differently. *Une Saison en Enfer* is like a shower of sparks, or rather flames, shooting out in all directions. But there is a basic theme, a progression, an inner logic. At the centre of the book is the conviction that mankind must be transformed — present man is something to be overcome.

Rimbaud's preoccupations, to 'change life' (*'changer la vie'*), to 'recover the lost paradise' (*'rechercher la clef du festin ancien'*), to redefine 'love' (*'l'amour est à réinventer'*), to find a way to a new world order *('Matin')* are all variations on traditional religious themes and place him firmly in the tradition of Pascal and even Saint Augustine (of the *Confessions*) rather than Lautréamont or Byron. *Une Saison en Enfer* is deadly serious : there is no place for humour, only occasional flashes of savage satire often directed against the author. Claudel described *Une Saison en Enfer* perfectly as *'un livre si sombre et amer, et en meme temps, pénétré d'une mystérieuse douceur'* ('a dark and bitter work, which is nonetheless suffused with a mysterious gentleness').

Many twentieth century critics were puzzled, not to say shocked, to find that the poet of revolt, *'le premier et le plus grand'* as Camus called him, should be so preoccupied with religion in *Une Saison en Enfer*.

In Rimbaud's early poems Christ is attacked as *'voleur d'énergies'* ('thief of human energy') especially sexual energy : he is responsible for turning healthy sensualists into guilt-ridden neurotics. As the anonymous heroine of *Les Premières Communions* puts it in a verse that must have profoundly shocked sensibilities of the time when it first saw print :

> *"Et mon cœur et ma chair par ta chair embrassée,*
> *Fourmillent du baiser putride de Jésus."*

"Both my heart and my body, embraced by your body, swarm with the putrid kiss of Jesus."

There is relatively little of this, however, in *Une Saison en Enfer* : here Christianity is attacked, socialist fashion, for being in perpetual alliance with the ruling classes, the nobles, colonialists destroying native cultures and so forth.

But there is another aspect to religion of which Rimbaud was well aware. The major world religions, Christianity and Buddhism especially, embody far-reaching attempts to remodel human nature : they can be seen as a protest and a revolt against the human condition. By comparison secular movements, with the possible exception of communism, are much less ambitious. Nineteenth century democratic and socialist movements accepted human nature as it was, and, if we go a little further back, we find that practically all the thinkers of the Enlightenment believed that there was a 'natural goodness' within mankind on which they could ultimately rely and a 'natural reason' to which they could appeal. Improved working conditions, electoral reform, free education, a higher standard of living &c. &c. would *automatically* change the individual for the better. As against this, Christianity teaches that man is a degenerate, fallen creature who can only be changed with the help of God, either by grace alone which is the Lutheran position, or by an intensive God-directed psycho/physical regime such as that devised by Ignatius Loyola for the members of the Society of Jesus. Neither of these procedures is 'natural' or inevitable.

Rimbaud, despite his recurrent outbursts against Christianity, was a good deal closer in his thinking to the pre-scientific religious view of man than the modern progressivist one, and, at least in *Une Saison en Enfer*, more consistently anti-rationalistic than anti-Christian — *"Je ne suis pas prisonnier de ma raison. J'ai dit Dieu"* ('Pagan Blood'). As far as he was concerned the Enlightenment had failed : he had the late nineteenth century results in front of his eyes and in his early poems he laments the wholesale trivialization and desacralization of life — *'notre pâle raison nous cache l'infini!'* ('pale Reason has blotted out the infinite!').

As for Christianity, it is not really a matter of whether it is true — who cares whether it's true or not? — but whether it actually works. And the reply is in the negative: Christianity, which promised 'a new heaven and a new earth' and a regenerated humanity, has not lived up to the vast expectations it aroused. It is not so much wrong as irrelevant. Rimbaud is not at all concerned with what humanity should be doing for Christ, but rather with what Christ should have done, and still be doing, for humanity, and in particular for himself — *'Pourquoi Christ ne m'aide-t-il pas, en donnant à mon âme noblesse et liberté? Hélas ! l'Evangile a passé !'* ('Why does not Christ come to my aid by endowing my soul with nobility and freedom? Alas! The Gospel has had its day'). This cry from the section *Mauvais Sang* has (probably deliberate) overtones of Christ's cry from the Cross, *"My God, my God, why hast thou forsaken me?"*

❖

Une Saison en Enfer is the record of a crisis (Louis Forestier, *Rimbaud*). What today we would call a 'psychological crisis' and what in the nineteenth and earlier centuries they called a 'spiritual crisis'. A crisis of belief at any rate.

Rimbaud, however, belongs to the modern era — one could justifiably call him a twentieth century thinker even though he died in 1891. In *Une Saison en Enfer* the belief system on trial is not Christianity, which as a system of ideas and moral imperatives accepted by most educated people went out in the mid-nineteenth century or earlier. But Rimbaud did not 'lose his faith' in the way in which so many Victorians did when they tried to square what the Bible said with Darwin: he seems to have had no *intellectual* (as opposed to emotional) difficulties in sloughing off Catholic doctrine as early as fourteen or so. His objection to Christianity, like Nietzsche's, was temperamental, 'spiritual' if you like — it was certainly not rational.

Une Saison en Enfer is clearly in some sense the chronicle of a 'loss of faith': it is the log-book of an explorer who finds that he has landed up in a land of spiritual and intellectual darkness instead of light. But the faith we see Rimbaud losing as the *carnet d'un damné* ('notebook of a condemned man') progresses is not Christianity but the pagan/magical anti-system that Rimbaud developed to replace at one fell swoop Catholicism and science.

For many people in the late nineteenth century faith in education and technology had effectively occupied the position vacated by organised religion. And nowhere was this truer than in France, France with its excellent public education system and its sceptical, strongly rationalistic literary tradition (Montaigne, Voltaire, Diderot &c.). Whereas the eventual leader of the English Revolution, Cromwell, was a fervent believer in God, Robespierre saw himself as the servant of Reason and even had her statue drawn in triumph through the streets of Paris. But Rimbaud, moving forward historically at breakneck speed, rejects with contempt the new sacred cows: they are just the same old wretched tricks and illusions under a different name — "old wives' tales and new arrangements of popular songs" as he describes the natural sciences and philosophy. Science, technology, democracy, education &c. &c. all these things had not changed the essential and so they are dismissed by Rimbaud as completely pointless. What is needed is radical, thorough and above all *sudden* change — Rimbaud is always in a tremendous hurry, he is *'pressé de trouver le lieu et la formule'* ('in haste to find the place and the formula [for changing the world]').

So where does that leave him? More precisely, where *did* it leave him in the two year period between the temporary closure of the Charleville *lycée* (where he had been a star pupil) because of the Prussian war and the publication of *Une Saison en Enfer* in October 1873? One possibility was political action, not the ballot-box social-democratic sort of action which was obviously far too slow, but a wave of revolutionary violence that would go through Europe like a tornado, sweeping aside the hated bourgeoisie — 'so respectable that they deserve to be burned alive' — and everything they represented for ever.

◆

The remarkable (untitled) poem '*Qu'est-ce pour nous, mon cœur, que les nappes de sang*' is usually dated 1871, the year of the Paris Commune, though whether it was written before or after the *semaine sanglante* (May 21 – 28) is unclear.

Since the poem is not particularly well-known, I shall give it in full along with a rough translation.

"Qu'est-ce pour nous, mon cœur, que les nappes de sang
Et de braise, et mille meurtres, et les longs cris
De rage, sanglots de tout enfer renversant
Tout ordre; et l'Aquilon encore sur les débris;

Et toute vengeance ? Rien! … — Mais si, toute encor,
Nous la voulons! Industriels, princes, sénats :
Périssez! Puissance, justice, histoire ; à bas !
Ça nous est dû. Le sang! Le sang! La flamme d'or !

Tout à la guerre, à la vengeance, à la terreur,
Mon esprit ! tournons dans la morsure : Ah!
Passez,
Républiques de ce monde ! Des empereurs
Des régiments, des colons, des peuples, assez !

Qui remuerait les tourbillons de feu furieux,
Que nous et ceux que nous nous imaginons frères ?
A nous, romanesques amis : ça va nous plaire.
Jamais nous ne travaillerons, ô flots de feux !

Europe, Asie, Amérique, disparaissez.
Notre marche vengeresse a tout occupé,
Cités et campagnes ! — Nous serons écrasés !
Les volcans sauteront ! Et l'Océan frappe…

Oh ! mes amis ! — Mon cœur, c'est sûr, ils sont des frères:
Noirs inconnus, si nous allions ! Allons ! allons !
O malheur ! je me sens frémir, la vieille terre,
Sur moi de plus en plus à vous ! la terre fond.

Ce n'est rien : j'y suis, j'y suis toujours..."

"What does it matter to us, my heart, the sheets of blood and the ashes and the thousand murders, the long cries of rage and all the acts of vengeance, the shrieks as all hell is let loose upon the world, and the North Wind howling across the wreckage?

Nothing. On the contrary, we wish it! Capitalists, princes, senators, perish! Authority, justice, history — no more! It is our due. Blood! Blood! The golden flame!

Put everything to the sword, unleash vengeance and terror everywhere, this is what I want! Let us bite back against our oppressors! Your time is over, republics of the world! Emperors, regiments, colonists, peoples, enough, I say!

Who is there to fan these flames into a mighty conflagration but us and those we consider our brothers? Join us, idealistic friends, you will find joy in all this. Never will we do any work, oh floods of fire!

Europe, Asia, America, disappear without trace! Our march of vengeance has swept all before it, cities and farmlands! — We shall be crushed! The volcanoes will erupt! The Ocean struck....

Rise up, my friends! I know in my heart that you are friends: unknown black people, join with us! Let us begin! Let us begin! O disaster! I feel my limbs trembling, the ground beneath my feet is shaking..... The earth itself is melting.

No; it is nothing; I am still here; I shall always be here..."

This is strong stuff. I remember reading it enraptured at the age of fifteen and reciting it out loud when my parents were out. It expressed perfectly the pent up frustrations and limitless resentments of youth...

Later, when I found myself close to the political action in Paris I felt differently. Not just because of fears for my own skin (though there was this) but also because I was no longer so sure that blood was 'the sacred flame' and that, if the moment came, I would be able to shed it so heedlessly as Rimbaud invites his 'brothers' to do.

An Islamic *jihadist*, presumably echoing the American phrase "wake up and smell the coffee" (i.e. 'get real'), or a similar Arabic slogan, said on television, "Now you know the smell of the coffee", with reference to the 7/7 suicide bombings in the London Underground. This is entirely in the spirit of *"Qu'est-ce pour nous, mon cœur"*.

◈

As it transpired, Rimbaud did not go down the path of terrorist action as the French anarchists Ravachol, Émile Henry and several others did during Rimbaud's own life time. Instead, during the period immediately after the Paris Commune, he opted for the path of individual, rather than social, transformation but on equally thorough, not to say fanatical, lines. A radical Marxist I knew in the Sixties (Chris Gray) talking to me about *Une Saison en Enfer* said that it was "an attempt at a purely individual revolution". "And of the inevitable failure of any such attempt", he immediately added.

I used at one time to assume that Rimbaud's for a while intense interest in magic, alchemy and esotericism belonged to an earlier, more 'adolescent' phase of his life (although he was only eighteen when he wrote *Une Saison en Enfer*), or, conversely, resulted from his disappointment with the collapse of the Paris Commune and the subsequent reaction. But, strangely enough, the famous *Lettre à Paul Demeny* where he develops his idea of the 'poet as seer' is dated May 15 1871, that is, while the Paris Commune was still in full swing though under sentence of death. Moreover, the letter opens with a (not particularly good) 'contemporary psalm' — as Rimbaud describes it — entitled *'Chant de Guerre Parisien'* ('Parisian War-Cry') all about the political situation in Paris. One should thus, perhaps, envisage Rimbaud's programme of personal transformation and literary revolution as all of a piece with the socio-political movement that was convulsing France — rather than as a transference of disappointed political hopes to the subjective sphere. During the so-called student revolution of May 68 in Paris I recall that there was a ferment of intellectual activity in and around the Sorbonne, not all of it by any means directly concerned with politics — though it was the exterior situation that was the indirect cause nonetheless. There seems to be something of this here.

◈

Rimbaud's programme for turning himself into a *voyant* ('seer', 'clairvoyant'?) is contained in two letters, one dated the 13th and the other the 15th May 1871. In the first, after ungraciously insulting his old teacher, George Izambard, who had been extremely useful to him, he writes

> *"Je veux être poète. Et je travaille à me rendre voyant… Il s'agit d'arriver à l'inconnu par le dérèglement de tous les sens. Les souffrances sont énormes, mais il faut être fort, être né poète, et je me suis reconnu poète. Ce n'est pas du tout ma faute. Je pense. On devrait dire : On me pense."*

> "I wish to become a poet. To this end I am striving to make myself into a seer. The idea is to reach the unknown by the disordering of all the senses. The sufferings involved are enormous, but you have to be strong, have to be born a poet, and that is how I see myself. It's not

my decision. It is false to say: I think. One should say: Someone is thinking through me."

The reference to Descartes' *'Je pense, donc je suis'* is interesting as it shows once again how Rimbaud rejects the entire Western individualistic, rationalistic tradition in favour of the older shamanistic one which sees the individual as the vehicle, voluntary or not, of superhuman forces. Instead of exercising free choice Rimbaud prefers to embrace his destiny ('It's not my decision'), instead of comfort he welcomes suffering and instead of self-assertion he calmly states that he intends to make himself into an instrument for powers unknown. Rimbaud proposes to take things further even than the pythoness of Delphi, since he is here offering to become, not simply a mouthpiece, but a thinking machine for another being (*'On me pense'*).

The second letter, addressed to Paul Demesny, says much the same though it starts off by recalling the 'Know thyself' of Greek humanism: *"La première étude de l'homme qui veut être poète est sa propre connaissance, entière; il cherche son âme, il l'inspecte, il la tente, l'apprend"* ('The first study of anyone who wants to be a poet should be understanding himself; he searches into his soul, inspects it, tests it, learns all about it'). But this is only preparatory: the real task, to adapt Marx's phrase, is 'not to understand oneself, as up to now poets and philosophers have been content to do, but to change oneself'.

> *"Je dis qu'il faut être voyant, se fair voyant.*
> *Le Poète se fait voyant par un long, immense et raisonné dérèglement de tous les sens. Toutes les formes d'amour, de souffrance, de folie : il cherche lui-même. Il épuise en lui tous les poisons pour n'en garder que les quintessences. Ineffable torture où il a besoin de toute la foi, toute la force surhumaine, où il devient entre tous le grand malade, le grand criminel, le grand maudit — et le supreme Savant! — Car il arrivera à l'inconnu! "*

'I say one must become a seer, must turn oneself into a seer.

The poet turns himself into a seer by a long, immense and systematic disordering of all the senses. He embraces all forms of love, suffering, madness: in these things he will find himself. He exhausts all poisons within himself, only keeping the refined extracts. Frightful torture which requires all his faith, all his superhuman strength, for he must become among other things the great sick person, the great criminal, the great damned soul — and the supreme man of knowledge. — He will reach what is as yet unknown! '

What is striking about this is the deliberateness of the project: it is the Will in the service of the Idea, Reason in the service of the Imagination. Becoming a visionary poet apparently requires the sort of training necessary to produce a Trappist monk or a candidate for the SAS. Most nineteenth century artists liked to see themselves as victims of malign Destiny and/or cruel Society, but only Rimbaud goes so far as to state that harsh treatment is essential and that, since he can't count on what will be meted out to him by others, he intends to oversee the programme himself. Other nineteenth-century artists talked airily of the 'disorder of the senses', but what they usually had in mind was some form of agreeable self-indulgence: it takes a Rimbaud to speak of a *systematic* disordering of the senses. One is reminded of the *Spiritual Exercises* of Ignatius Loyola, which were deliberately designed to be a kind of spiritual third degree — even today Jesuit novices undergoing the course not infrequently go to pieces as letters to the Catholic magazine *The Tablet* testify.

'Why all this? What's the point? Won't something less strenuous work just as well?' one might ask in bewilderment.

The answer is no it won't. Because the basic human material is of such poor quality, it needs to be thoroughly shaken up, 'deranged', because only in this way can one get results. *'Quel travail ! Tout à démolir, tout à effacer dans ma tête !'* ('What work needs to be done ! Everything must be demolished, all that is in my head wiped out!')

◆

Rimbaud, rather surprisingly in some ways, does not envisage himself as a sort of poetic Messiah (or Antichrist) ushering in the new era by his very existence: he claims to be quite content with the much humbler role of pioneer psychic explorer, the equivalent on the poetic/visionary plane of those medical researchers who drank down cholera infected water in order to test the germ theory of disease. Moreover, Rimbaud anticipates that he will fail but cheerfully dismisses this as of no consequence since others will come after him and 'begin at the very horizon where he has collapsed'.

Rimbaud's programme for poetic and psychic self-development is not a personal power kick which explains why he can with a clear conscience launch into these far-fetched aesthetic theories at the very moment when the future of the socialist revolution is about to be decided with bayonets in the streets of Paris. He identifies the poet with Prometheus *('le poète est vraiment voleur de feu')* and Prometheus we must remember was punished not for pride like Lucifer but for being a benefactor of the human race. In this same letter to Paul Demesny Rimbaud speaks of the poet as *'chargé de l'humanité'* ('responsible for humanity') and envisages poetry not as a mere 'reflection' of what is going on but as preceding and initiating change *'La poésie ne rhythmera plus l'action; elle sera en avant'* ('Poetry will not just keep pace with action, but will be in advance [of action]'). It is not surprising that, given this extremely ambitious vision of the role of poetry in the future society, Rimbaud subsequently showed not the slightest interest in literature as a mere career.

◆

Where does the poet/visionary get his stimulus from? Not God certainly; but not from humanity either. At this stage in his life Rimbaud adheres fairly closely to the Romantic 'religion' that goes back at least to Rousseau: the source is what we would call 'the unconscious' but it is not the individual unconscious which is why he says (on two occasions) *'Je est un autre'* meaning, not that he is 'just anyone', but that he is 'a vehicle for someone or something'. This was the original meaning of 'inspiration', i.e. being 'breathed into' (by a god). The origin of the poet's visions thus lies in what today we would today call the 'collective unconscious' — though even this is still too limited a conception since it is restricted to the human sphere. Rimbaud himself speaks of *'l'âme universelle'*, 'the World-Soul'. In a formula as significant and much more useful than the far better known one about the disordering the senses, Rimbaud defines the poet's role: *'Le poète définirait la quantité d'inconnu s'éveillant en son temps dans l'âme universelle'* ('The poet's task is to give expression to the unknown element that is awakening during his epoch within the world soul').

The focus and ultimate aim of all this project is, however, restricted to *this* world: it is not a flight into another dimension. This is why he writes, without any implied slight, *'Cet avenir sera matérialiste, vous le voyez'* ('This future will be a materialistic one, you will see it for yourself').

◆

The idea of changing the individual by intensive psycho/physical training has a long history since it goes right back to the age of shamans and 'holy men'. Monasticism is essentially a continuation of the same in a communal single-sex environment: the vows of lifelong 'Chastity, Poverty and Obedience' are today denounced as unnatural and inhuman but that is precisely the point. Nature, left to itself, will not produce either the Nietzschean Superman or the Christian anti-Superman, the saint. The last two and a half thousand years, in both West and East, have witnessed a sustained, by and large sincere, but ultimately unsuccessful attempt to provoke what one might call a human mutation. The desired end product, the Christian saint or Buddhist *Bodhisattva*, is a human being in whom altruistic feelings have entirely replaced the biological ones of self-preservation and self-aggrandisement. Rimbaud understood this well enough — "The saints! Titans! Heroes! Where can they be hiding? Stylites, anchorites, aesthetes of the Holy Grail whose talents no longer find employment!" Compared to the pedestrian and money-grubbing nineteenth century bourgeois these people obviously had something to recommend them.

◈

Educated people who look down on mysticism, ESP, the paranormal, occultism and so on, fail to understand that the movement is a counter-current produced by the material advances of the last century: it is a frantic last-ditch attempt to hit back before it is too late. Science and technology devalue the human individual completely since a human being is, physically and mathematically speaking, no different from any other 'body' — a baby thrown off the Leaning Tower of Pisa falls at the same rate as an empty beer can or a slug (excluding air resistance). Magic, however, is a human based technology, the source of power being the magician's personal will — and you do not need money or social connections or a college education to develop will power. Also, you can start the inner transformation immediately: there is no need to hang about like the Marxists endlessly waiting for the appropriate 'historical conditions'.

◈

Rimbaud anticipated modern hippies, drop-outs and rebels without a cause by nearly a hundred years: he grew his hair long, smoked hashish, refused to get a job, scrawled *'Mort à Dieu'* in chalk on public benches at Charleville &c. &c. But the Sixties and Seventies youth revolt was in general anything but controlled; Rimbaud's ambitious plans to make himself into a seer are more in line with the ideas of Carlos Castaneda and the various 'programmes of personal development' that flourished for a while in the USA such as EST and Neuro-Linguistic Programming.

It is unclear how far Rimbaud actually went with his own programme. Nonetheless, there was from the beginning a hard, self-willed, ascetic, streak in Rimbaud's character, which marked him out from the run of the mill happy, go lucky bohemian and which he presumably inherited from his mother. Louis Perquin, who knew her personally, described her as *"une femme inflexible; je ne l'ai jamais vue rire ou sourire une fois'* ('An inflexible woman; I never saw her laugh or smile once').

◆

Délires II relates the complete collapse of Rimbaud's programme of self-transformation: instead of turning himself into a visionary poet, he has, as he now sees it, very nearly turned himself into a lunatic.

And yet *Une Saison en Enfer* is not the record of failure. Certainly, Rimbaud has not found the 'key to the primeval feast' but he is no longer looking for it. If his aim all along was to escape from Hell, *Une Saison en Enfer* is a success story, the account of a mission very nearly completed. Although Rimbaud has not yet left Hell in the final section *'Adieu'*, he considers his release to be imminent: *'Je puis dire que la victoire m'est acquise: les grincements de dents, les sifflements de feu, les soupirs empestés se modèrent'* ('I am confident that ultimate victory will be mine: the gnashing of teeth, the hissing of flames, the pestilential moans diminish with every hour').

Rimbaud is contemporary enough to envisage Hell as essentially a state of mind rather than a place: he says in *'Matin'*, 'I believe I have now concluded the account of *my* hell'. In modern terms he has managed to work through the accumulated experiences of his youth and, without the help of a priest or psychoanalyst, has rid himself of them for good — *'Tous les souvenirs immondes s'effacent'* ('The pathetic episodes of my past life fade into nothingness'). He has made the irrevocable decision to change his whole style of life which, in his case, means amongst other things saying farewell to art — *'Une belle gloire d'artiste et de conteur emportée!'* ('A brilliant career as artist and novelist nipped in the bud!').

Rimbaud stands at the end of *Une Saison en Enfer* a 'free man', psychologically free (because freed of his past) and he would have regarded this as the essential point. Of course, the actual use to which he put this 'freedom' and whether the latter part of his life as a clerk in Aden or arms-trafficker in Abyssinia was any improvement on Rimbaud the social revolutionary and Charleville *enfant terrible* is another matter. But he *did* break with all his bohemian and literary acquaintances, *did* leave Europe, *did* stop writing for good, *did* cease to interest himself in religious or philosophic theories and, most important of all, apparently ceased to see himself as 'a damned soul'. His subsequent concerns in life were entirely practical: instead of counting the number of syllables in a line of poetry he counted sacks of coffee beans and instead of spending his time wondering what was wrong with humanity we find him writing an account of the topography of Abyssinia for the French equivalent of the *Royal Geographical Society*. It is typical of the 'new Rimbaud', one might almost say the 'born-again Rimbaud', that he writes in one of his letters from Harar "if I had a son I would not want him to become an artist but an engineer".

◈

Since *Une Saison en Enfer* has a happy ending of sorts, are we to suppose that Rimbaud has gained some sort of liberating insight during his traumatic experiences? If this is so, the place to look is not in *Mauvais Sang*, the longest and best known section, but in the enigmatic *L'Impossible* where Rimbaud tries to get to the root of the sickness, his own and that of the entire West.

L'Impossible functions as a hinge within the overall structure, or, to change the metaphor, as the Aristotelian *peripeteia* ('turnabout'), the moment when the action completely changes direction because of some unexpected piece of news. In Greek tragedy *peripeteia* means change for the worse, as, for example, when the Messenger in *Oedipus Rex* unwittingly reveals to Oedipus that he is the killer of his own father, thus precipitating the death of Jocasta and Oedipus' self-blinding. But in comedy it is possible to have an unexpected change for the better as here.

Up to this point the general tone has been one of desperation. The untitled Prologue tells us that the author has lost for ever his previous state of innocence, his place at the 'primeval feast'. *Mauvais Sang* records the narrator's various unhappy reincarnations as rebel, victim or outcast, while *Nuit de l'Enfer* gives a graphic picture of the torments of Hell, physical and mental. *Délires I* introduces us to the widow, apparently the narrator's only companion and supporter, but he considers her untrustworthy and unworthy of his confidences. *Délires II* is the story of the narrator's own pitiful delusions and self-deceptions, as he now sees them. This brings us to *L'Impossible*. But, although *L'Impossible* ends on a temporarily sombre note — *'Déchirante infortune !'* ('Heart-breaking misfortune!') — from here on the work becomes much calmer, more positive, and ends on a quietly triumphant note which one would hardly have expected half-way through.

Has Rimbaud found some new method of changing life? When asked precisely this by the widow in *Délires I* he replies in the negative — he is only looking for it. *L'Impossible* brings the realisation that the situation is a good deal worse than even he had originally thought. It is not just a matter of getting rid of the guilt-ridden ethos of Christianity: there is something inherently wrong with the entire West, which has lost contact with the 'original and perennial wisdom'. What, then, is this wisdom? It is, seemingly, the Zen-like message that 'things are as they are': the problem is thinking there was a problem in the first place. *'L'homme se joue, se prouve les evidences, se gonfle du plaisir de répéter des preuves, et ne vit que comme cela ! Torture subtile, niaise, source de mes divagations spirituelles'* ('Humanity is playing a game with itself, insists on proving the obvious, swells up with self-satisfaction at repeating endlessly the same proofs, and is incapable of living in any other way ! A complicated and childish form of torture which is at the root even of my own spiritual confusion'). So all this soul-searching, which has filled all the previous sections of *Une Saison en Enfer* is now seen to be completely pointless; the moment has come to 'say goodbye to all that' and Rimbaud does just this three sections further on in *Adieu*.

Rimbaud has not seemingly received any kind of profound intuition about the nature of the universe and man's place in it: his 'enlightenment' turns out to be the realisation that 'a rose is a rose is a rose....' But that is precisely the point. One is reminded of the Zen story about the Patriarch of a monastery asking his monks to write a poem to show their understanding of Buddhism and promising to nominate the monk who writes the best poem as his successor. The head monk, whom everyone expects to succeed as Patriarch, writes a quatrain comparing the mind to a mirror and exhorting everyone to keep it clean all the time so that no dust can cling to it. The Patriarch praises the poem publicly but in private tells the author that there is much he does not understand. Another monk overnight posts a poem anonymously in the corridor; it states that the 'natural mind' does not need polishing because there is nothing to which the dust can cling. The Patriarch, who knows there is only one person in the monastery who could possibly have written it, secretly confers his begging bowl and robe on this monk who at the time worked in the kitchens and was little thought of by the others. He eventually becomes the famous Zen master, Hui-neng *.

The difficulty, however, is that once one starts thinking about 'being natural', one's effort gets in the way and the mirror becomes clouded. This seems to be what Rimbaud is saying in *L'Impossible* : the ceaseless rationalising which he considers to be typically Western is a sort of Original Sin from which there is no escape. One thing that

---

* The story is recounted by Alan Watts in his book, *The Way of Zen*, pp. 111-112.

can be done, however, is to leave off thinking and pass on to action : the very next section, *L'Eclair*, is concerned with work (manual work). It is perhaps worth mentioning here that Zen was the first Buddhist school to require all its monks to perform manual work.

However we rate this insight on the religious/philosophical plane, i.e. as triviality or profound truth, it seems to have worked for Rimbaud. In the next three sections we leave soul-searching and return to strictly mundane concerns: the problem of employment in *L'Eclair*, of realisable social progress in *Matin*, and of Rimbaud's personal plans to leave Europe in *Adieu*. The world has not changed in any miraculous fashion — as the widow in *Délires I* believes that it can 'thanks to the magic powers' of her little friend — nor is it likely to. However, Rimbaud is no longer quite so bothered.

Enlightenment is, after all, nothing special — "I obtained not the least thing from unexcelled complete awakening, and for this very reason I knew it to be unexcelled, complete awakening" (attributed to the Buddha).

In *Matin* Rimbaud states that he has concluded his account of his sojourn in hell — the first time he has even suggested that he might be leaving the underworld at all. He still has some desires for a better society — why should he not have? — but he neither affirms nor denies that the longed-for change will come about. He merely asks *when* "will we salute the beginning of a new concept of work, a new form of wisdom....?" Moreover, this new world, if it comes at all, is not a religious apocalypse, quite the reverse, since it will signal the 'end of superstition' and will be the 'first time' that humanity really 'celebrates Christmas on this earth', as opposed to the countless times when it has celebrated the birth of the false Messiah, as Rimbaud sees him. The last line can be interpreted as an attack on all otherworldly doctrines and expectations — *'Esclaves, ne maudissons pas la vie!'* ('Slaves, let us not curse [the gift of] life !')

In the last section of all, *Adieu*, Rimbaud reinforces the moral of a return to *this* world and the day to day. *'Moi qui me suis dit mage ou ange, dispensé de toute morale, je suis rendu au sol avec un devoir à chercher et la réalité rugueuse à éteindre !'* ('I who considered myself to be a magician or angel, beyond the reaches of good and evil, have had to come down to earth and realise that I have a mission to accomplish and must embrace harsh reality'). On this note he steps out to greet the new era, which, for a brief moment, almost looks like Russia after 1917 seen through the eyes of a recent convert to Bolshevism.

◈

The irony is, of course, that now he has decided to 'live from day to day' and no longer search for the formula for transforming humanity, Rimbaud finds that he needs his iron will and extremely tough constitution, not in order to become the poet/seer who will help to usher in the new era, but simply in order to stay alive.

Byron and Shelley could afford to travel in carriages and stay at inns if they wished. But when 1875 Rimbaud walked alone through Switzerland he arrived at Milan in such bad shape that a local woman took pity on him and lodged him for a while. He pushes on towards the south but suffers sunstroke near Livorno and is repatriated by the French authorities. In 1877 we find him being repatriated by the French Consulate of Stockholm, but once back in France he embarks for Alexandria. There he falls ill and is forced to beat a retreat to Charleville for the winter season. And so it goes on. Exposure to the subtropical sun and a hard life generally soon took a toll on Rimbaud's youthful looks — *'une beauté du diable'* according to Verlaine — and in the Harar photograph, one of the few we have of Rimbaud, he looks like someone who has been in the Foreign Legion for the last ten years which in a sense he had.

Whereas Gauguin ended up in lush Tahiti and took beautiful native mistresses, Rimbaud for some reason ended up in Aden, *'un roc affreux, sans un seul brin d'herbe….la chaleur est excessive'* ('A frightful rock without a blade of grass… the heat is stifling'). The poet who wrote at the age of sixteen

"Chair, Marbre, Fleur, Vénus, c'est en toi que je crois"

would have found little enough of these at Aden.

Rimbaud was not really an arms-trafficker: he did sell a shipment of arms in Abyssinia to King Menelik but most of the time he spent in North Africa he was dealing in coffee and sitting at a desk or standing behind a counter. His travels sound a good deal less romantic when we realise that he was often ill; eventually, he had to be shipped back to Marseille in 1891 to have his right leg amputated and he died later that year at the age of thirty-seven after frightful sufferings.

All this is not only depressing but rather odd. Rimbaud never really was a *'poète maudit'* while he actually wrote poetry: to be received at once by the most fashionable poets in the country is every young writer's dream. However, as an explorer and adventurer he really does seem to have been jinxed: although one of the first to penetrate into the heart of Abyssinia this did not bring him any renown and his chief independent trading exploit, the Menelik arms deal, brought in very little considering the enormous effort and dangers involved (his two European associates in the venture died during the trip). It is as if, once he had renounced the idea of being a 'damned soul', he became instead a 'damned man'.

◆

"L'amour est à réinventer"
(Délires I)

A LOT OF PEOPLE today seem to imagine that Rimbaud made up for poverty, obscurity and hardship by an extravagant sex life. Would that he had! But *'l'orgie et la camaraderie des femmes m'étaient interdites'* ('Orgies and the friendship of women were forbidden me') as he notes wryly.

Delahaye, Rimbaud's closest Charleville friend, recounts a rather sad incident that happened when Rimbaud was sixteen or seventeen. Rimbaud, doubtless feeling that it was high time he put into practice the hedonistic principles expressed in *Soleil et Chair*, wrote a letter asking for a rendezvous with a certain Charleville young girl of good family. She duly arrived at the agreed place, the Square de la Gare, but accompanied by her maid. Rimbaud, tongue-tied, was unable to make any conversation and had to endure not only the young beauty's scorn but the titters of the servant girl. And the following day Rimbaud's mother received a letter from the girl's father asking Vitalie Rimbaud to keep a better watch on her son.

According to Delahaye, Rimbaud enlisted in 1871 as a volunteer in the 'federal forces' and was, at the age of sixteen, stationed at the barracks in Babylon, Paris. Here, it has been suggested, he was sexually molested, possibly gang-raped. The story seems perfectly plausible: we have a good-looking young boy fresh from the provinces being thrown in with a horde of desperadoes who expected either to be dead or sent to Cayenne by the end of the month. Even if things did not go as far as this, the disturbing poem *Le Coeur Volé* is clearly the record of a profoundly traumatic incident — though it may have saved his life for it prompted a sudden return to Charleville and so he missed the *semaine sanglante* when up to 17,000 persons, mainly civilians, were summarily executed.

Although Rimbaud moved for a while in bohemian circles in Paris, rather surprisingly, there don't seem to have been any young women amongst them. And there would certainly have been no available French (or native Moslem) women in Aden where Rimbaud spent most of his time while in North Africa; this may have been one reason for his move to Harar where he lived for a year or more with a native girl, Argoba. I had always assumed that the girl was a true 'native' untouched by Western civilization in the style of Gauguin's adolescent mistresses in Tahiti. However, on re-reading a biography of Rimbaud, I find she was Catholic, dressed in European clothes and 'liked smoking cigarettes'! Rimbaud, far from imbibing 'primitive wisdom' from her, apparently did his best to educate her and at one point even thought of enrolling her in a convent school! Rimbaud sent her back to her parents just before he embarked on his Menelik arms-dealing expedition either because he had tired of her, or for her own safety and protection. This seems to have been the only on-going relation Arthur Rimbaud ever had with a woman.

◈

The piece which seems to me to be the most revealing with regard to Rimbaud's emotional and sexual make-up is the haunting *Les Déserts de l'Amour*. Since, like *Qu'est-ce pour nous, mon cœur*, it is not that well known, I give it complete in a fairly literal translation.

"Without a doubt it is the very same countryside. The same rustic house belonging to my parents: the same hall with the paintings of shepherdesses above the doors, the coat of arms, the lions. We have dinner in the drawing-room with the brown wainscoting. The dining-table is very large, set out with candles and wine. And the servants! There were very many of them, as far as I can remember. — One of my young friends was present, a priest and dressed in the habit of a priest: he claims it enables him to be freer. I clearly remember his room, which was purple with panes of yellow waxed paper; then there were his books, hidden away, that had been soaked in the ocean!

As for me, I was left to my own devices in this endless country mansion: I see myself reading in the kitchen, drying my mud-spattered clothes in front of the fire while I can hear people talking in the next room. The sound of milk being poured in the morning moved me to tears like the sound of night falling, and all this took place in the last century.

I am in a very dark room: what am I doing? A servant woman comes up close to me; all I can say is that she was like a little dog; and yet she was beautiful, for me she had a maternal nobility beyond words: pure, familiar, charming, so charming! She pinched my arm.

I cannot exactly recall her face: but how well I remember her arm, I held the skin between my fingers. And her mouth that my mouth seized like a hungry little wave, a wave throwing itself endlessly against the shore. I pushed her over into a basket full of cushions and sailcloth lying in a dark corner; all I can remember are her drawers with their fringes of white lace.

Then, dreadful to relate, the wall behind us turned into the vague shadow of a tree, and I was plunged into the lovelorn sadness of the night.

This time, it is the Woman I saw in the town. I spoke to her, and she to me.

Once more I am in a room without light. Someone came to tell me that she was in my room ; I saw her in my bed, she was there for me, and the light was out! I was profoundly moved, all the more so because it was the family home. Suddenly I felt ashamed because I was in rags and she who was so well-dressed was giving herself to me; she ought to leave there and then ! Deep distress filled me, I lifted her up and let her fall outside the bed, almost naked; and overcome with unspeakable weakness I fell on top of her and dragged her along with me amongst the carpets in the darkness. I could see the reddish light carried about by a member of the family in the neighbouring rooms. Then the woman disappeared. I shed more tears than God could ever demand of anyone.

I walked out into the never-ending town. O Misery! I was drowning in the darkness of the night, searching for my lost happiness. It was like a winter's night, snow was falling, enough snow to smother the whole world. I shouted up to my friends, 'Where has she gone?' but they replied evasively. I found myself in front of the glass doors of the place where she goes every evening; I ran into the garden now buried under the snow. Someone pushed me away. I cried and cried because of what had happened. In the end I hid in a dusty basement, and seated on the beams I let the tears flow out of me all that night. — And always my tiredness returned to me each day.

I saw that she had returned to her life of everyday, and that the offer of love would take longer to repeat itself than a star. She did not return, and never will return to me, the Adorable one who came that night into my room — and that I never presumed would do so. — It is the simple truth, that night I cried more than all the children in the world."

This piece is extremely significant both psychologically and stylistically.

Dreams are of no more than passing interest, in life and in literature, unless they embody archetypal figures in archetypal situations. Now here we certainly do have an archetypal situation, that of the young boy and older woman (mother figure). But it is an unusual and interesting variation on the theme. Generally we have the young boy helplessly aspiring after a beautiful older woman who is unapproachable, thus a sense of rejection and unworthiness. But here it is the young male who, from timidity, refuses the advances of an older woman above him socially — "I was in rags while she was elegant". Instead of subsequently feeling guilty for accepting the advances of a mature woman — and blaming her for it — as all too often happened in bourgeois nineteenth century society, the narrator here feels guilt for not having had the courage to seize the chance offered. This shows a very different Rimbaud from the usual one, much more vulnerable emotionally and carrying around a very different kind of guilt from the disquiet Rimbaud occasionally feels about the consequences of his revolt against God and society.

Whether the story was based on a real incident does not matter too much: it was certainly deeply felt and Rimbaud obviously identifies himself with the speaker. My own impression is that it is based on dreams Rimbaud actually had, but not a real incident. For one thing, the Rimbaud farmhouse at Roche was hardly the elegant mansion with many servants described in the first paragraph. It has been suggested that Rimbaud got the idea for the story from reading the *Confessions* of Jean-Jacques Rousseau who came from very lowly circumstances and actually *was* seduced by a Countess whom he saw as a mother figure — he even called her 'Maman'.

Stylistically, this is one of the first pieces where Rimbaud uses surrealistic devices, which he was to develop in *Les Illuminations*. The 'story' consists of two dreams, one about a country house and the other a town house though the dream country house is, we are told, based on a real house belonging to the narrator's parents. The abrupt transitions, especially in the second dream, make the piece all the more effective and anticipate film techniques. But there is no need to introduce completely irrational and senseless details like the priest's books 'having been soaked in the ocean'. I also think it weakens the story to speak of all this happening 'in the last century' — it is removing what happens from the realm of reality-based dream to the realm of complete fantasy. However, these are minor faults. In general the two crucial scenes are realistically described: we can see in front of us, as in a film by Renoir or Resnais, the servant girl thrust into the basket full of cushions and sailcloth and, later on, the two figures half-naked in the darkened bedroom lying on the carpet with a 'reddish' light (paraffin lamp presumably) being carried around in an adjoining room.

In *Les Illuminations* Rimbaud goes much further in the direction of surrealism, or irrealism, but for this very reason none of the pieces in Rimbaud's last work have the directness and simplicity of *Les Déserts de l'Amour*.

◈

Rimbaud's encounters with people relatively uncontaminated by the West were not, however, wholly disappointing. In his later years Rimbaud became greatly attached to his young (male) adolescent servant, Djami, who accompanied him on the Menelik expedition and from there back to Aden where Rimbaud had to be hospitalised. Rimbaud mentioned Djami on his deathbed and bequeathed 3,000 francs to him, a small fortune. Unfortunately Djami died before receiving the money though his young wife and child did receive it.

Some commentators have conjectured that this was a homosexual relationship but there is no evidence for this and Rimbaud's business associates, after his death, dismissed the idea. It was perfectly normal, indeed practically obligatory, for a European in Africa at the time to have at least one male servant.

This brings us to the celebrated relationship with Verlaine. I do not think it important either way whether Rimbaud was or was not 'really' homosexual: the private lives of artists do not necessarily shed any great light on their works and certainly do not make the works either better or worse aesthetically. Still, since sex had such an extremely important part in Rimbaud's thought and writings, the question is worth discussing at least cursorily.

I doubt if anyone would imagine that Rimbaud was other than heterosexual just from reading his poems — and, with one or two rare exceptions, they were not intended for publication so he would have had no particular reason to conceal his true inclinations. Also, if Rimbaud really had been mainly homosexual, one would have expected other French writers to have subsequently hinted, or at least written in their private diaries, that they had had relations with the fascinating and at the time good looking boy of seventeen who subsequently became so famous. As far as I know no one ever has. That there was an extensive gay milieu at the time we know from Proust and other authors: the Baron de Charlus, one of the main characters in *À la Recherche du Temps Perdu*, was based on a real person, the *fin de siècle* dandy Robert de Montesquieu. My impression, for what it is worth, is that the sexual element in Rimbaud's relation with Verlaine was not that great — this goes some way to explaining its neurotic intensity since sex gives some sort of emotional release. There are definite sado-masochistic overtones in the account given in *Délires I,* but the 'torture' seems to have been more psychological than physical and it is the widow (Verlaine) who is on the receiving end. Rimbaud himself certainly had self-punishing, masochistic tendencies but I cannot see him actually acquiescing in being beaten by someone else: he was the dominant one of the pair Rimbaud/Verlaine in every way (except where money was concerned). It seems that the Parisian bohemian milieu, which came to shun Rimbaud, blamed him rather than Verlaine for the scandal even though Rimbaud was a minor and was technically the victim since he was shot at by Verlaine in Bruxelles.

◆

> "Si Dieu m'accordait le calme céleste, aérien, la prière — comme les anciens saints!"
>
> ('Mauvais Sang')

SINCE RELIGION bulks so large in *Une Saison en Enfer* (or so at any rate I would claim), we might ask whether Rimbaud was in any sense Christian. The short answer to this, despite all that Claudel and others have written, is, no.

I did not know this when I started this personal re-evaluation of Rimbaud, but the priest in charge of the Catholic Mission at Harar is on record as saying that Rimbaud should have become a monk. Henriette Célestin (*'Le Temps' 10/6/33*) reports Mgr Jarosseau as saying to her personally: *"Nous [de la Mission] disions qu'il avail manqué sa vocation et qu'il aurait dû se faire trappiste ou chartreux"* ('We used to say at the Mission that Rimbaud had missed his vocation: he should have entered the Trappist or Carthusian Order'). Now, Rimbaud's sacrifice of an artistic career does make one think of the pagan convert burning the idols he had once worshipped — Isabelle Rimbaud declared that Rimbaud literally burned copies of *Une Saison en Enfer* in her presence — and Rimbaud's self-imposed hardships remind one of acts of penance. As for solitude and silence, Rimbaud certainly had plenty of that and seems to have coped well enough. Note that the priest cites what are probably the two most austere Catholic Orders.

Rimbaud undoubtedly had the 'religious temperament' but this is not the same thing as having religious belief — though in an age of faith like the Middle Ages the two would normally have coexisted in the same person. What do I mean by 'religious temperament'? Negatively, it translates itself as profound dissatisfaction with material existence, however privileged or favourable, and positively as a strong sense that there is a greater reality beyond the physical. In the last two centuries disbelief has been gaining ground remorselessly and, from the Romantics onwards, people with a religious temperament (as I define it) have tended either to be extremely hostile to organised religion (Shelley, Nietzsche, D.H. Lawrence &c.) or at the very least have found it difficult to subscribe to a religious faith for intellectual reasons. On the other side, leading figures of the established Christian Churches, with one or two notable exceptions, have been singularly lacking in the religious temperament and have been desperately trying to turn Christianity into a reasonable sort of creed which emphasizes good works in this world. In so doing they have succeeded in making Christianity more socially acceptable but have stripped it of everything specifically religious. I was amazed to hear an eminent retired bishop say publicly that he was "suspicious of anyone who claimed to have had a religious experience" (his very words).

So far so good. If he had been born in the Middle Ages Rimbaud would almost certainly have ended up in a monastery: after all, the most famous troubadour of his time, Bernard de Ventadour, ended his days in the Cistercian Abbey of Dalon and the same Abbey subsequently received another troubadour, the notorious Bertrans de Born, who spent twenty years in the cloister. But monasticism is a style of life, not a belief system. Rimbaud's particular religious tendencies did not incline him towards Christianity as such: its strange mixture of the human and superhuman repulsed rather than attracted him. He almost always speaks of Christ slightingly and his concern in *Une Saison en Enfer* is with God, not Christ. He does not write, *'J'attends Christ avec gourmandise'* but *'J'attends Dieu avec gourmandise'*. What is Christianity anyway? If we consider its central theological doctrine to be the atonement, i.e. St Paul's claim that Christ 'died for our sins' and thus saved us from Hell and the Devil, then there is no trace of Christian belief in Rimbaud's writings, nor any suggestion that there ever could be. In the quotation at the head of this section, Rimbaud cries out for *'calme céleste'* ('peace of mind'), not forgiveness of sins.

If not Christianity, what then? I have argued that, in *L'Impossible*, Rimbaud's position is very close to that of Zen Buddhism. But Rimbaud was far too sombre a character to have settled permanently for Zen as a religious philosophy. His temperament required a belief system, which stresses the radical 'otherness' of God while nonetheless affirming some possibility of mystic union with the Absolute. Sufism would have suited him perfectly had he been brought up within an Islamic, rather than Christian, cultural environment. Rimbaud did ask his mother to send him out a French translation of the *Koran* but it has been well said that the only thing Rimbaud took from Islam was the idea of *kismet*, i.e. fatalism.

◈

"Quand irons-nous saluer la naissance du travail nouveau?"

('Matin')

WAS RIMBAUD in any sense a socialist writer? If we consider the main trait of socialism to be a concern with the poor and the downtrodden, then the answer is, somewhat surprisingly, in the affirmative. Rimbaud's first published poem was *Les Étrennes des Orphelins* which is full of genuine sentiment, not Victorian sentimentality. While the leading Parisian poets, including Verlaine, were writing about gardens and evening breezes, the adolescent Rimbaud was writing revolutionary calls to arms like *Le Forgeron* ('The Blacksmith') celebrating the capture of the Tuileries in 1791 or the magnificent *Les Mains de Jeanne-Marie* where the archetypical nineteenth-century Romantic Goddess figure fuses with that of the revolutionary activist:

> *"Elles [les mains] ont pali, merveilleuses,*
> *Au grand soleil d'amour chargé,*
> *Sur le bronze des mitrailleuses*
> *À travers Paris insurgé!"*

> "Marvellous to relate, her hands have grown pale in the blazing sunlight charged with love, on the bronze of machine-guns in the midst of Paris in revolt!"

There are several references to the victims of colonialism and to the savage repression of the Paris Commune in *Une Saison en Enfer* and the sentiments are certainly sincere. To deliberately hold out his hand to black people, as he does in *'Qu'est-ce que pour nous, mon cœur'* — *"ils sont des frères, noirs inconnus…"* ('They are our friends, unknown black people') — and even identifying with them by saying, *'Je suis...un nègre'* as he does in *Mauvais Sang* would surely have been without parallel at the time even within progressive circles. *Démocratie*, from *Les Illuminations*, is a devastating propaganda piece, all the more telling because the words are put into the mouth of a *colon* who has no illusions about the civilising mission of *la Belle France* :

> *"Le drapeau va au paysage immonde, et notre patois étouffe le tambour.*
>
> *Aux centres nous alimenterons la plus cynique prostitution, nous massacrerons les révoltes logiques."*

('The flag flies high above the filthy landscape, and our patois smothers the sound of the drum beat.
  In the town centres we introduce the crudest form of prostitution. We wipe out all justified revolts.')

Although *Une Saison en Enfer* starts off as an exclusively personal document, the ending is a call to arms which suggests, with hindsight, the storming of the Tsar's palace in Saint Petersburg in 1917:

> *"C'est la veille. Recevons tous les influx de vigueur et de tendresse réelle. Et à l'aurore, armés d'une ardente patience, nous entrerons aux splendides villes."*

('We are on the threshold of a new era. Let us all absorb influxes of strength and tenderness, and at dawn, armed with burning patience, we will enter the splendid towns.')

Rimbaud's apocalyptic style of socialism, with its twin emphasis on social and personal revolution, was by no means unique in nineteenth century France. As Jacques Droz recounts in the fourth chapter of his very interesting study *Europe Between Revolutions 1815-48*, although the socialist movement in France lagged well behind that in England during the same epoch in terms of influence and practical achievement, France remained the intellectual capital of Europe where the most advanced doctrines of social and political emancipation flourished. A succession of thinkers, Saint-Simon, Fourier, Proudhon, to name only three amongst many, proclaimed that the bourgeois order of competition and the exploitation of man by man was shortly to be replaced by a Golden Age of harmony and true individualism. To Fourier, the idea of the 'free association of working men and women' was a principle quite as important and far-reaching within the social and economic sphere as Newton's Universal Attraction had proved to be within the inanimate world. Although Fourier did not live to see them, one or two phalansteries were actually founded in France and as far afield as Russia and America (though they did not last long). Similarly, in what were, at the time, extremely widely read works, *Le Livre du Peuple* and *De l'Esclavage Moderne*, Lamennais, who combined communism with primitive Christianity, delivered the typically Rimbaudian message that "it was in men's minds that social regeneration had to take place first of all" (Droz, p. 78). At around the same time, Weitling, a German born tailor who spent much of his life in Paris, attained quasi-messianic status within the international working-class movement. He anticipated Marx (who detested him personally) by proclaiming that the working class was destined to become the spearhead of universal emancipation leading to a new epoch of peace and concord for humanity.

Towards the close of the century, more practical concerns ousted such millenarian hopes, partly because trade unionism was becoming a force in society, and in consequence more respectable, and partly because of the fierce opposition of Marx and the Marxists to 'utopian' modes of thought —although Marx himself as a young man had been caught up in very similar movements in Germany. The same broad current of idealistic socialism surfaced temporarily within the 'Arts and Crafts Movement' in England and, Oscar Wilde, of all people, penned a perfectly serious essay *The Soul of Man under Socialism* as a sort of utopian socialist manifesto. (After a century of world wars, enforced collectivization in Russia and Cultural 'Revolution' in China, it makes rather painful reading.)

◈

To what extent did Rimbaud put any of this into practice? This is an embarrassing question for out and out hero-worshippers of Rimbaud since his post-literary career was hardly socialist in any sense of the word. I do not think a genuine revolutionary would even have accepted the job of foreman on a Cyprus building-site: during the self-same period middle-class Italian and French socialists and anarcho-syndicalists got jobs on the factory floor in order to radicalize the workers and unleash strikes. Worse still, Rimbaud does not seem to have been an easy person to work under: the story of him throwing a stone at a workman and accidentally killing him comes from a trader, Ottorino Rosa, who would have had no apparent reason to invent it. That Rimbaud had an unpleasant streak of gratuitous violence seems to me undeniable and, if we treat *Délires I* as, in part, an account of his liaison with Verlaine (as I do), he was himself well aware of the fact. On the other hand, both Rimbaud's employers and the priests at the Catholic Mission at Harar seem to have thought highly of his moral character. *Veritas in media res* ('Truth lies somewhere in between').

◈

"Je me flattai d'inventer un verbe poétique accessible, un jour ou l'autre, à tous les sens"
('Délires II')

WITH THE BEST will in the world French poetry often appears tame when compared to English. It is the poetry of the Age of Reason. Part of the fault undoubtedly lies with the limitations of the alexandrine, the twelve-syllable line used by the vast majority of French poets and dramatists that all too often

"Like a wounded snake drags its slow length along"

as Pope puts it beautifully. If neatness and tidiness are what one wants, alexandrines in couplets are perfect, but it requires all the skill of Racine to get some tragic intensity or even variety of expression into the form. The fatal tendency is to pause at the end of each couplet and, not only that, to pause after the first rhyme as well, so the poem has, as it were, to be cranked up at the beginning of every single line. This effectively puts paid to working up any dramatic momentum or developing a complex train of thought.

Rimbaud himself commenced his poetic output with couplets of alexandrines, which he handles with quiet assurance in *Les Étrennes des Orphelins*. Since the subject is the misery of orphan children, we don't want rapid movement and the constraint of the verse form is actually an advantage since it stops the poem falling back into sentimentality.

In *Ophélie* Rimbaud stretches out the already extended alexandrine as far as it can possibly go, once again with complete appropriateness since the verse in itself suggests the clothes of Ophelia spread out on the surface of the water.

"— Et le Poète dit qu'aux rayons des étoiles
Tu viens chercher, la nuit, les fleurs que tu cueillis;

> *Et qu'il a vu sur l'eau, couchée en ses longs voiles,*
> *La blanche Ophélia flotter, comme un grand lys."*

Note that the deliberately English form *'Ophélia'* (instead of *'Ophélie'*) provides an extra syllable and thus stops the rhythm falling into a regular 'ti-tum-ti-tum...' However, this is a quatrain with alternate rhymes, not a pair of rhyming couplets, and on closer examination the length of the lines turns out to be variable (*11-12-12-11*) as it is throughout the poem — though one does not notice this at first which is a tribute to Rimbaud's skill and judgment. Already, at the age of fifteen, Rimbaud is composing "in the sequence of the musical phrase not in the sequence of the metronome" (Pound, *Imagisme*) but he is doing it so discreetly that you do not notice any irregularity.

However, when we come to what is intended to be a full-scale manifesto of romantic paganism (or pagan romanticism), *Soleil et Chair*, the alexandrine couplets are clearly beginning to be a dead weight. The opening two lines

> *"Le Soleil, le foyer de tendresse et de vie,*
> *Verse l'amour brûlant sur la terre ravie"*

appear rather trite — which is the last thing one would expect from Rimbaud. The poem has a certain decorative finish like a porcelain plate but one feels that the verse form and diction tone down the deeply felt sentiments in a way that the author did not really intend. It is a bacchanal painted by Claude Lorraine: all the more interesting for the contrast between manner and message but not entirely convincing as a romantic call to arms.

The obvious way to loosen up the alexandrine is to reduce the number of end-stops and vary the position of the break in the middle of the line, as Hugo does incessantly. In *Le Bateau Ivre*, however, this would not be appropriate, as we require a persistent forward thrust, suggesting the current of the water. Rimbaud brings off what is virtually the impossible: he end-stops practically all the lines and yet communicates a sense of irresistible forward movement, never allowing the verse to fall back, and this for twenty-two quatrains one after the other with only a slight pause between verses, until the rhythm does finally quieten down as the ship (which is the speaker of the poem) finally stops and reflects on its enormous voyage.

One has only to contrast lines where Rimbaud piles up words pell-mell to suggest the confusion of the ship in full course

> *"Glaciers, soleils d'argent, flots nacreux, cieux de braises !*
> *Echouages hideux au fond des golfes bruns"*

with the completely different rhythm near the end when the ship is no longer moving

> *"Si je désire une eau d'Europe, c'est la flache*
> *Noire et froide où vers le crépuscule embaumé…"*

to see how perfectly Rimbaud suits rhythm to sense.

It is worth noting that Rimbaud achieved his first public success with *Le Bateau Ivre* by reciting it at a gathering of Parnassian poets. Rimbaud's poetry is at its best read aloud.

Generally, it would seem that French poets, prior to the modern era, were mortally afraid on the one hand of being too declamatory and, on the other, of writing poems that were barely indistinguishable from songs. Rimbaud moves in both directions. In *Le Bateau Ivre* he shows it is possible to be declamatory without being pompous even though he uses strange and complicated words. And in the poems cited in the section *Délires II* that he refers to as *'des espèces de romances'* ('ballads'?) he has no qualms about using forms based on the style and rhythm of popular songs. In fact there is practically no verse form or style that Rimbaud is not capable of handling with absolute confidence; he even anticipates contemporary 'Rap poetry' in the technically brilliant pieces collected together in his *Album Zutique* such as:

JEUNE GOINFRE

Casquette
De moire,
Quéquette
D'ivoire,
Toilette
Très noire,
Paul guette
L'armoire,

Projette
Languette
Sur poire,

S'apprête
Baguette,
Et foire.

(To translate this is beyond me.)

Rimbaud had no need to develop 'free verse' as such since he had developed a much richer and more adaptable *genre*, what one might call the 'prose symphony' or 'concerto'. Ezra Pound's valiant attempt to expound his ideas about life and the world in a 'liberated' verse form (in his *Cantos*) is, apart from one or two set pieces, a resounding failure. It falls between two schools, being neither 'poetry' in the traditional sense of being musical and imaginative, nor prose in the sense of being precise and informative. Rimbaud's achievement in *Une Saison en Enfer* is the opposite of this.

◆

It is ironic, to say the least, that, in his aesthetic theorising, Rimbaud always stresses the visual element since his strong point is not ultimately imagery but mastery of sound and rhythm. Many of Rimbaud's 'ballads' and 'romances' are cabaret *chansons* as they stand — 'lyrics' in the original Greek sense. The prose of *Une Saison en Enfer* and the best of *Les Illuminations* is full of the most subtle sound patterns, harmonies, alliterations, echoes, solo riffs, orchestral groundswells.... Sections of *Une Saison en Enfer* and *Les Illuminations* could literally be transposed into music just as they stand and they would make complex and fascinating sound patterns. Rimbaud does not so much write as compose in words. It is rarely true that sentences in prose appeal even if one has not the slightest idea what they mean. But take a sentence chosen at random on opening Rimbaud's 'Complete Works':

"Enfant, certains ciels ont affiné mon optique : tous les caractères nuancèrent ma physionomie. Les Phénomènes s'émurent."

One feels that one does not even need to know what this means: it still means something — like music.

It is here that we see Rimbaud's Catholic upbringing bearing fruit: his prose, situated, as it is halfway between song and statement, recalls liturgy or Gregorian chant. The principal difference between prose and poetry is that in poetry there is a much closer connection between sound and sense: poetry is meant to be *heard*. This was also true of the King James Authorised Version: it was intended to be *read aloud* in Churches for a largely illiterate population and this is doubtless one of the reasons why it is so successful as a piece of writing.

◈

It is an important point that Rimbaud's writings, both verse and prose, are extremely easy to memorise — something that is rarely true of modern poets. I knew a midwife from a working-class Parisian suburb, little given to reading at all, who told me she used to recite to herself

> *'Oisive jeunesse*
> *A toute asservie*
> *Par délicatesse*
> *J'ai perdu ma vie'*

when walking down the steps of her dismal HLM (Council Estate) on her way to work. *"Tu vois, c'est tellement joli!"*. While Auden appealed to socialist middle-class intellectuals, Rimbaud's poems, and some of Verlaine's also, actually *did* appeal to 'ordinary people'. The taste of the general public in poetry, and to a certain extent in music as well, remains unashamedly romantic, *kitsch* if you like, but I have no problem with this — I have myself swelled the numbers of those congregating in Hyde Park to listen to Pavarotti singing *Nessun Dorma*.

Apart from turning out lyrical poems that are very easy to learn off by heart, Rimbaud also excelled in producing highly memorable one sentence formulae, some of which have already become more or less proverbial such as *'L'amour est à réinventer'* ('Love needs to be re-invented') or *'Il faut être absolument moderne'* ('It is necessary to be absolutely modern'). The ability to produce pungent brief formulae and slogans is typically French : there would perhaps never have been a French Revolution if J-J Rousseau had not written the resounding (but ultimately rather meaningless) sentence, "Man is born free but is everywhere in chains". And the spirit of Arthur Rimbaud must have been haunting the corridors of the Sorbonne in May 68 since many of the slogans plastered on the walls, such as *'La révolution sera une fête ou ne sera pas'* ('The Revolution will be a festival or will not take place at all'), or, *'Prenez vos désirs pour des réalités'*

('Treat your desires as realities') were so Rimbaudian I seriously wondered whether they had not been recently unearthed in some previously unknown fragment. (The most successful of these slogans in reality came from the pen of Guy Debord, the leader of the Situationists.)

◈

"Une belle gloire d'artiste et de conteur emportée!"

('Adieu')

Une Saison en Enfer is the only work, apart from one or two early poems, that Rimbaud took the trouble to have printed. Was it, or was it not, his farewell to literature?

    Isabelle Rimbaud, the poet's sister, recounts, long after the poet's death, that he had literally burned in front of her eyes the entire shipment of copies of *Une Saison en Enfer* received from the Belgian printer. This is usually dismissed today as fabrication, especially since the greater part of the print run was found thirty years later mouldering in the basement of the *Alliance Typographique, 37 de la Rue aux Choux, Bruxelles* by a Belgian investigative lawyer. And as for stopping writing altogether, it now seems very probable that many of the prose poems eventually published (without Rimbaud's knowledge) as *Les Illuminations* were written after the printing of *Une Saison en Enfer* (which we can date exactly). So quite a few editors conclude, quite wrongly in my view, that *Une Saison en Enfer* did not in fact constitute a decisive break with art and literature.

    Actually, even though Isabelle Rimbaud was not an entirely reliable witness, since, as a devout Catholic, she was eager to 'whitewash' her brother as much as possible, it seems to me quite likely that Rimbaud really did burn one or two copies of *Une Saison en Enfer* at the family farm. He certainly made no attempt to recover the rest of the print run by paying what he owed — and he could surely have done this at some stage during his later life. People don't seem to realise that burning your own works is, or was, quite common amongst young aspiring authors who either get disappointed at not becoming a sensation overnight or genuinely come to the conclusion that what they have been writing is complete rubbish. A friend of mine at Oxford one day announced to us that he had (literally) burned his whole poetic output. I myself not only did the same but around the age of thirty staged a much more extensive *autodafé* when I burned not only the accumulated writings of several years but also books, diaries, even clothes — in fact I kept the bonfire going on and off for a whole week, adding to it day by day! A volume of Rimbaud was, as a matter of fact, one of only two French books to survive the holocaust (the other one was *Manon Lescaut*).

What in fact is remarkable about Rimbaud's 'burning of the manuscript' is not the occurrence itself but the quality of what was very nearly lost to the world and, secondly, that Rimbaud actually kept to what he said. My Oxford friend, for example, eventually became a successful science-fiction writer and has during his career published at least one collection of poems. But not only did Rimbaud, during his subsequent life, not show the faintest interest in getting published but he even completely stopped *reading* anything literary or philosophical. A list of the books he asked his mother to send him when out in Harar makes somewhat hilarious reading. Top of the list is *L'Album des Sciences Forestières et Agricoles* closely followed by the *Livre de Poche du Charpentier* — 'The Encyclopaedia of the Agricultural and Forestry Sciences' and 'The Carpenter's Handbook'.

Delahaye, who was Rimbaud's closest Charleville friend, recounts that one evening when Rimbaud was back from his travels he dared to ask him whether he still thought 'about literature'.

> *"Il eut alors, en secouant la tête, un petit rire, mi-amusé, mi-agacé, comme si je lui eusse dit : 'Est-ce que tu joues encore au cerceau?' et répondit simplement : 'Je ne m'occupe plus de ça'."*

> "He shook his head with a little laugh, half-amused, half-irritated, as if I had asked him whether he still played with

a stick and hoop. He ended up by simply saying, 'I don't bother with such things any more'."

What, then, of *Les Illuminations?* I must admit that I do not have anything like such a high opinion of these prose pieces as most editors and readers do. They seem to me of very uneven quality: some like *Solde* and *Génie* are fabulous pieces of imaginative writing, but others are just jottings with the odd striking phrase, and one or two such as *Mouvement* are best forgotten entirely. With some exceptions, which will be discussed in a moment, they strike me as being the sort of thing that one writes out of habit, by reflex action as it were. I have often noticed that when someone has taken a decision to give something or someone up for good, there is a brief period of apparent backsliding before the final break. This is what I see happening here. So, from my point of view, there is no particular problem about some of the pieces dating from the year *after* the printing of *Une Saison en Enfer* : this does not mean that Rimbaud went back on his famous rejection of literature.

Of course, in the nineteenth-century the systematic exploration of the unconscious, likewise the use of drugs that stimulate the imagination, was in its infancy at least amongst serious authors, so the endless parade of fantastic images we find in *Les Illuminations* was much more significant at the time. Nonetheless, I am sure that if Rimbaud had prepared the volume for publication he would have pruned a good deal of these prose poems, dismissing many of them as exactly the sort of 'magical tomfoolery' he had denounced in *Délires II*.

Take a few images at random from *Les Illuminations*

1. *'la Lune entendit les chacals piaulant par les deserts de thym'*
2. *'Madame *** établit un piano dans les Alpes'*
3. *'Je serais bien l'enfant abandonné sur la jetée partie à la haute mer'*

4. *'Je suis le piéton de la grand'route par les bois nains; la rumeur des écluses couvre mes pas'*

Now **(1)**— 'The Moon hears the jackals howling in the deserts of thyme' —does nothing to me at all. **(2.)** is rather more striking — 'Madame *** is setting up a piano in the Alps'. But again my reaction is basically, 'What if she is?' **(3.)** on the other hand ('I could be the child abandoned on the jetty swept out to sea') is, to me at any rate, marvellously evocative, and **(4.)** ('I am walking down the great avenue with the dwarf trees; the sound of sluice-gates closing covers my steps') is masterly in terms of image, sound and psychological resonance.

Possibly, you do not feel the same about these images, will be struck by ones that do not strike me, and vice-versa. This, however, shows the vulnerability of this kind of writing and indeed of the entire surrealist style : it depends in a rather haphazard way on the particular experiences and sensibilities of the reader. Myths and folk-tales depend on this as well, of course, but the successful ones have an extended, general human appeal — the others have been weeded out over the centuries in a sort of natural selection process for archetypes.

What does point to a late date for some of the pieces of *Les Illuminations* is the amazing mastery of sound patterning which is more developed even than in *Une Saison en Enfer*. Take for example

"Les voix instructives exilés... L'ingénuité physique amèrement rassise... Adagio. Ah! l'égoïsme infini de l'adolescence, l'optimisme studieux : que le monde était plein de fleurs cet été! Les airs et les formes mourant... Un chœur, pour calmer l'impuissance et l'absence! Un chœur de verres de melodies nocturnes... "

I shall not translate this as the sound and a vague idea of what the writer is writing about is all that is needed, and seemingly all that Rimbaud wishes to communicate.

One can, however, see this extraordinary facility becoming a disability rather than a spur to further endeavour. The above does not, at the end of the day, have anything particular to say. At first one assumes that Rimbaud is making some point about the political situation (*'les voix instructives exilés'* makes one think of the French political activists forced into exile after 1871) but Rimbaud gets bored with this theme and abruptly drops it. There is still an underlying 'sense' to be found in *Les Illuminations* but it is evaporating fast, and this is certainly not a good thing. Not only is Reason becoming increasingly divorced from Imagination, but the latter is degenerating into mere Fancy, to use Coleridge's critical terms.

Since some at least of *Les Illumiantions* are later than *Une Saison en Enfer*, we should maybe ask whether there are any pieces in this collection that show a further development of Rimbaud's thought.

There are certainly two or three pieces, which relate directly to sections of *Une Saison en Enfer* and the themes that are prominent there. *Vagabonds* deals, in twenty or so lines, with the Verlaine/Rimbaud liaison — or rather conflict — which has been the substance of *Délires I*. Thus, we see Rimbaud desperately trying to convert his backsliding companion to his own pagan beliefs, *'de le rendre à son état primitif de fils de Soleil'*. There follows a brilliant *haiku*-style summary of their life together — *'et nous errions, nourris du vin des cavernes et du biscuit de la route, moi pressé de trouver le lieu et la formule'*. ('Thus we wandered about, drinking the wine of caverns [water] and feeding on road biscuit, while I was all the time in haste to find the place and the formula'). This thumb-nail sketch incidentally underlines that the essential conflict between Rimbaud and Verlaine was not emotional or sexual but what one might call ideological.

This piece, excellent though it is, nonetheless adds nothing new though it does pinpoint issues that were perhaps obscured in the relevant section of *Une Saison en Enfer*. Similarly, although one would not want to be without the prose poem *Départ*, it is simply a summary of the final section of *Une Saison en Enfer, Adieu*.

There are, however, at least four pieces, which suggest a completely new departure in Rimbaud's thinking, namely *Après le Déluge, Royauté, Solde* and *Génie*. In the first Rimbaud re-introduces or rather revamps the earlier theme of the regeneration of humanity, which is the central issue in *Une Saison en Enfer*. But, philosophically, the idea that there is going to be a second deluge which will bring forth a 'new heaven and a new earth' is thoroughly unconvincing and Rimbaud obviously does not even believe it himself: it is basically a device to enable him to download onto the reader a lot of striking images, perhaps originating in drug induced visions. Although one might just about conceive of a 'new order' being brought about either by a world-wide political or, alternatively, 'spiritual' revolution, one cannot possibly conceive of this coming about via a new deluge — this is simply science fiction, and not even very interesting science fiction. Other vistas of the future are more intriguing, such as the various sketches of future *'villes'* and the inhabitants thereof, but it is never entirely clear whether these modernist cities are supposed to be desirable or undesirable — and as far as I am concerned I would like to know.

Royauté shows that Rimbaud has modified the attitude he took in *Délires I* towards his own self-intoxication and delusion. A man presents himself to the crowd and says of the woman he has with him, "I want her to be a queen!" And, significantly in the context of Rimbaud's life, *'Il parlait aux amis de révélation, d'épreuve terminée'* ('He spoke to friends of a revelation, of a period of testing that had ended'). Surprisingly, instead of dismissing this would-be prophet as a charlatan, Rimbaud goes on to say, *'En effet ils furent rois toute une matinée ....et tout l'après-midi'* ('And in effect they *were* king and queen during a whole morning... and a whole afternoon'). So Rimbaud's period when he believed himself to be a seer and precursor of a future golden age was not entirely invalid: it was true while it lasted, had its own authenticity. This is a more mature evaluation than the Rimbaud of *Une Saison en Enfer* was capable of, or interested in, making.

Solde is a strange and brilliant piece which one is not sure how to take. On the one hand, it looks like a violent attack, some hundred years or so ahead of its time, on a society dedicated to turning absolutely everything into merchandise, including Rimbaud's own dreams of a regenerated humanity and of personal liberty — since in this vast clearance sale even *'l'éveil fraternal de toutes les energies…'* ('The fraternal awakening of all energies…') and *'l'anarchie pour les masses'* ('anarchy for the masses') are up for grabs. But is the poem really a satiric comment on neo-capitalism and its levelling of all non-materialistic values? Rimbaud makes the whole enterprise sound extremely liberating: it is a sort of *potlatch* of the aspirations of a whole civilization and one is tempted to say, "If that's what it's like, carry on".

This brings us to *Génie*, the most affirmative and optimistic piece Rimbaud ever wrote. Rimbaud has, in his writings, repeatedly condemned Christ as a false prophet since he has not ushered in a new era and has deluded humanity with promises of imaginary future bliss. But the 'genius' of whom Rimbaud speaks, a sort of pantheistic 'Holy Spirit', or Bergsonian *'élan vital'*, does not promise anything and above all does not become incarnated as a human being. Rimbaud remains to the end thoroughly hostile to the very idea of the incarnation, of the divine manifesting itself as a human being. *'Génie'* does not apparently need to do anything at all : it is enough that 'he', or 'it', exists. 'He' will not depart to another world, will not 'redeem' man's sins and take revenge on the wicked *'car c'est fait, lui étant, et étant aimé'* ('All this is done simply by him existing and being loved [by us]').

What are we to make of this conception in practical terms? *Génie* is something more than wishful thinking but stops short of being a firm prophecy of what is to come. It is interesting to see Rimbaud returning here to the Romantic conception of a force or principle which is neither human nor truly superhuman, neither circumscribed within Nature nor fully transcendent. What is *Génie*?

> '*Il est l'affection et l'avenir, la force et l'amour que nous, debout dans les rages et les ennuis, nous voyons passer dans le ciel de tempête et les drapeaux d'extase.*'
> ('He is affection and the future, the strength and the love that we, standing amidst our angers and troubles, see passing across the stormy sky and in the flags of ecstasy.')

◈

"Il faut être absolument moderne"

('Adieu')

WHAT WOULD Rimbaud be doing today? For a start I doubt if he'd be a writer at all. Why not? The interpretation I am putting forward in this little book is that Rimbaud was basically someone who wanted to change the world and humanity, and that he gave up literature because he realised this was not the way to go about it (and maybe the attempt was doomed in any case). During the early 19th century, writers, and especially poets, were enormously influential figures: Byron, a best-selling author and idol of the crowd if ever there was one, "bestrode Europe like a colossus" and Pushkin, in his own country, was not far behind him. The Polish poet Mickiewicz openly cast himself in a messianic nationalist role — the examples can be multiplied endlessly. If not quite the "unacknowledged legislators of the world" as Shelley described poets in his *Defence of Poetry*, the Romantic poets of the first half of the 19th century shaped not only sensibility but political and social attitudes to an unprecedented degree: indeed, it is astonishing how little subsequent cultural European movements have been able to add to their legacy.

However, by the time Rimbaud was emerging from his Charleville lycée into the glare of world history, the balance had already tipped in favour of scientists, engineers and mathematicians as the men of the moment. Rimbaud himself realised this, hence his rather pathetic wish, expressed in a latter to his mother, that "if I had a son I would want him to be an engineer". Certainly, a contemporary Arthur Rimbaud, if he did deign to write at all, would be hostile to the entire *'poète maudit'* bit, just as he was dismissive in his own lifetime of the French Byron, de Musset. I did as a matter of fact know a Rimbaudian figure in the Latin Quarter in Paris during the Sixties, a French Algerian poet by the name of Belghanem. He made a point of saying, "I've never read a word written by Arthur Rimbaud, and never intend to".

Rimbaud, the precocious Charleville schoolboy, would today have been guided towards theoretical physics or mathematics rather than Latin and French literature (Rimbaud was a good Latinist). I can see Rimbaud as a brilliant young mathematician who, having made a reputation for himself, would then publicly declare that mathematics was complete rubbish. A few years ago there was an article in the *New Scientist* about a noted young French mathematician who now lives as a recluse in the country and has nothing whatsoever to do with mathematics. The American ecological terrorist known as the Unabomber was at one time seen as a promising mathematician and did research at Berkeley before taking to the woods (quite literally).

If involved in computers, Rimbaud would either take the extreme AI stance like Marvin Minsky (who claimed that in a few years time advanced computers would "treat us human beings as household pets"), or the equally extreme anti-AI stance, or, more likely, both at different periods of his life.

Would Rimbaud have started a religious cult ? In some ways he had the temperament for it and certainly I can see him leading a heretical religious movement in the Middle Ages. But now? Somewhat surprisingly in a way, considering his vast ego, Rimbaud, even at the height of his '*voyant*' period, never cast himself in the role of saviour or superman : he claimed only the much more modest and certainly more thankless status of a precursor and pioneer.

Politically, despite the young Rimbaud's genuine sympathy with the poor and downtrodden, Rimbaud today would almost certainly be more on the Right than the Left — inasmuch as these terms have any meaning now — if only because, within the intelligentsia at least, socialism of one sort or another has been almost an article of faith for the last hundred years. Rimbaud was a compulsive rebel and anything that smacked of the official line or political correctness would have irritated him beyond measure. He would doubtless be somewhat ambivalent in his attitudes towards terrorists, just as he was ambivalent in his own lifetime in his attitudes towards hardened criminals. Unable to applaud fundamentalist Islam, Rimbaud would probably say that the decadent West "deserved nothing better".

◈